# A TASTE OF
# *INDIA*

## DELICIOUS VEGETARIAN RECIPES
### For Body, Mind and Spirit

## By Bibiji Inderjit Kaur

*Foreword by Yogi Bhajan*

**Arcline Publications**

*Pomona / Berkeley*

A TASTE OF INDIA
Delicious Vegetarian Recipes for Body, Mind and Spirit

Edited by Dayal Kaur Khalsa
Executive Editor - Dharm Darshan Kaur Khalsa
Cover art and illustrations by Siri Gian Kaur Khalsa
Typesetting by Highpoint Type & Graphics, Inc.

Published by Arcline Publications,
A division of the Kundalini Research Institute,
Pomona, CA (714) 623-1738 / Berkeley, CA (415) 644-3229

ISBN 0-89509-051-1

*This book is dedicated to my beloved husband and children for whom I have always loved to cook the foods they most enjoy.*

*Acknowledgements:*

I would like to thank my sons, Ranbir Singh Bhai and Kulbir Singh Bhai, and my daughter, Kamaljit Kaur Kohli, for their inspiration and energy which made this book possible.

Also, I would like to thank Sardarni Guru Meher Kaur for her hours of selfless efforts to complete this book. I am also grateful to Sardarni Raminder Kaur for her assistance and contribution.

Thanks also to all my sisters in divine, those beloved friends and family members, who helped to kitchen-test these recipes.

# Cooking Is a Key
# To the Joy of Life

*Cooking is an art of life and a science of health. If we love our bodies, minds and selves, we will love to keep them alive and healthy. By eating food which gives us maximum energy we can stand balanced against the outside pressures and the inside traumas.*

*Wonderful cooking is cooking that can keep us young, energetic and able to face every event in life with perfect self control and self posture.* Cooking is a key to the joy of a cozy life.

*Cooking does not mean just cooking with fire. Cooking means keeping the fire of life going through enjoyment of the warmth, coziness and love of the Beloved, immersed in the dance of Shakti and Shiva.*

*The science of cooking is the art of happiness — personal, social and communicative. The delight of cooking and its wonderful taste evoke from within us our best civilized behavior. The enjoyment of cooking brings about the enjoyment of sharing the coziness of life. It is productive and satisfying to the body, mind and soul.*

— Yogi Bhajan

# Contents

# The Cook as Healer

The traditional Indian healing system teaches that food is medicine. Along with balanced physical exercise such as the practice of yoga, and a positive mental attitude which can be achieved through meditation, the food we eat is one of the three great pillars of total health.

The master Indian cook is really a holistic healer. He or she ministers to the needs of the whole person — body, mind and spirit. Simple food and herbs are the materia medica. Not only are the ingredients and nutritional values of food of great importance for good health, but so are its color, taste and smell. When her child has the flu, a mother will prepare special spicy "chapatis" to break the fever. A creamy turmeric drink may be served for stiff joints, or a diet of well-cooked beans and rice may be prescribed for a digestive weakness. While the ingredients in these dishes are believed to have curative properties in themselves, equally important is the love with which they are prepared and the spirit in which they are served. Through love and service, the Indian cook imparts healing energy to those who partake of a meal.

The traditional Indian diet is purely lacto-vegetarian. No meat, poultry, fish or eggs are included. It is naturally low in fats, cholesterol and uric acid. Simple vegetarian food is referred to in Indian scriptures as "sattvic bhoj." "Sattvas" means pure essence. "Bhoj" means food. A person who eats sattvic food is likely to be more calm, mentally agile and clear thinking than one who eats heavier foods. The hot spices used in Indian cooking are said to have a "rajasic" quality. This means that they stimulate sexual energy, which is also the drive to create and achieve. Rajasic foods, taken in moderate amounts, are considered to be useful for people who work, or who practice a rigorous discipline such as Kundalini Yoga or martial arts. It is believed that through work, exercise and spiritual discipline, sexual energy is transmuted into other forms of creative expression. "Tamasic" foods, such as animal products and alcoholic beverages, are said to dull the mind and lead to sloth and regressive behavior.

Another aspect of the traditional Indian diet is that it includes a moderate amount of protein from wheat, dairy products and rice-bean combinations. Indian medical tradition would say that the Western diet is dangerously high in protein. (The average American consumes about three times as much protein as is recommended by the World Health Organization.) Protein, compared to the other food groups, is relatively hard to digest. Too much protein in the diet puts an unnecessary burden on the liver and other organs.

The Indian diet is composed of pure and simple foods — unrefined, unprocessed and natural. While in recent years foreign influences have led to a greater use of canned foods, bleached white flour and refined white sugar, traditional Indian cuisine uses only fresh foods, unbleached flour and unrefined sugars. The recipes in this cookbook reflect the more traditional diet while bowing to the modern necessity for ease of preparation. Thus, canned or prepared foods have been used when they do not severely detract from the taste or healthfulness of the dish. Since unrefined sugar is difficult to obtain in the West, other natural sweeteners have been substituted.

As you will see, Indian cooking relies heavily on several main ingredients. A closer look at them will help to explain why Indian food is so healthful:

Rice. A native crop of India, where it has been grown since the beginning of recorded history, rice is rich in B vitamins and iodine. It is a high quality protein which is easily digestible and non-fattening. Rice with curried vegetables is very good for the kidneys, for blood purification and for muscle development. I recommend basmati rice, an unpolished white rice from India, or Texmati rice, its North American equivalent.

Wheat. Appropriately named the staff of life, whole wheat is an excellent source of B vitamins and minerals. In the form of bread, of which India has many varieties, it is known as a brain food. When cooked with fruits, nuts, herbs or spices, it can be used for medicinal purposes. The wheat grown in the mineral rich soil of Punjab, in northern India, is among the most healthful foods in the world.

Dairy products. Indian cooking uses dairy products which are simple and easy to digest. Yogurt is rich in vitamin B-12 which is essential for the nervous system. Since the body cannot manufacture this vitamin from vegetable sources, yogurt is an important element in vegetarian nutrition. Yogurt neutralizes acidic conditions and enriches intestinal flora. For health purposes, homemade yogurt is much better than the store bought kind. "Panir" is a simple cheese made from whole milk which has been curdled, drained and compressed. It is lower in fat and easier to digest than cottage cheese or hard cheeses. "Ghee" is clarified butter, that is, butter with all the milk solids and impurities removed. It is the oil of choice in traditional Indian cuisine since it is highly regarded as a nutrient and a preservative. It can be heated to a higher tempera- ture than butter, is lower in cholesterol, yet has a deep, rich taste. It will keep unrefrigerated for weeks.

*Legumes.* The family of legumes, or "dahl" as it is called in India, includes beans, peas, lentils and so on. These foods are useful in enriching the hemoglobin content of the blood. Combined with rice, wheat or corn, they form complete proteins which are easily digestible.

*Herbs and spices* give Indian food its distinctive flavor. Nearly every herb or spice has its medicinal properties; however, a few of them are used so frequently that they are worthy of special mention. *Onions* are known as blood purifiers. They have been prescribed for a long list of ailments including colds, flu, earaches, dizziness and a variety of stomach ailments. *Garlic* has been called a natural antibiotic. It is used for gastrointestinal disorders, typhus, cholera and bacterial infections. *Ginger* is soothing and strength- ening to the nervous system. It is good for backaches, fatigue, fevers, bronchial coughs, and it stimulates digestion. *Turmeric* has been recommended as a means of keeping joints flexible and skin and mucous membranes in good order. Recent research indicates that it may be useful in preventing diabetes and cancer. *Chiles,* green and red, including cayenne and crushed red pepper, are high in Vitamins C and A. Despite their hot and pungent taste, they are very soothing to the system. They are good for circulation and digestion and prevent constipation.

A complete list of ingredients and their medicinal properties would, in themselves, fill the pages of this book. Combining the ingredients into delicious dishes designed to correct specific condi- tions is an art in itself. A good experiment for the beginner is to ask yourself how you feel after you've eaten a well-prepared Indian meal, or better still, how do you feel after you've made Indian vegetarian cookery an important part of your diet! I hope that your experience with this cookbook will yield very satisfying results.

For more information on the healing properties of food, you can read *Foods for Health and Healing*, by Yogi Bhajan, available from this publisher.

*Cookery and Culture:*

# Devotion in the Kitchen

Food, family, devotion and community. The meanings of these words are intertwined in the vast cultural tapestry of India. They are the precious links of a golden chain binding humankind to God and God to His creation. A saying on the wall of a "langar" hall — the community dining room attached to a Sikh temple — reads, "Food and drink are the gifts of God. Service and devotion are contributed by his servants."

It is with this awareness that an Indian cook approaches the preparation of a meal: that it is a privilege to take part in the continuing act of nurturing creation through the art of cooking. What constitutes a well-balanced meal in India is a mixture of protein and carbohydrate, taste and aroma, beautiful presentation, devotion and love.

On the earthly plane, cooked food provides tangible evidence of the workings of the law of "karma," the cycle of cause and effect. We work all week — be it in the office, on the farm or in the home — to earn our daily bread. That is the cause. The effect is the eating and enjoying of our food. When we eat, we feel that we've earned it!

Another aspect of the law of karma can be expressed in the traditional saying, "For what men give, they shall receive. And for every gift that is given, an offering shall be required." God, the giver, provides food to nourish humankind. Human beings, in turn, are obliged to use the strength imparted by food to serve others. Thus, life on earth is an experience in community: the immediate community of family, the life of the neighborhood, and then the community of the spiritual person in relation to God — all mutually serving each other. In this spirit, over two hundred years after that saying was painted on the wall of the langar hall, Mahatma Gandhi wrote to his disciple, the English woman Mirabhain, "Eat your food thankfully and keep yourself fit for service."

Eating together might be called the "yoga" of family life. For it is in this simple, daily activity that the various members of the family get yoked (yoga) together in one harmonious experience. A meal prepared with love, served in an atmosphere of grace, and eaten with thankfulness brings together the physical and spiritual aspects of life. In India, where, for the most part, it is still the man who works outside the home and the woman who works inside, meal time expresses the essence of the mutually nurturing qualities of traditional family life. It is a time and space for each member of the family to gracefully play out his or her role. The meal is tangible proof of the man's ability to provide for his family, a way for the woman to creatively express her love for her family, a place for the children to feel nurtured and to express their gratitude for being cared for so well. It is a time when the lines of communication bypass the petty irritations of the day to deal directly with the essentials of human-being-ness. Heart speaks to heart, soul speaks to soul, and all via the stomach, of course!

It is just this undeniable physicality of eating — everyone has to do it to live — that makes food such a wonderful vehicle for building community. In Indian life, among friends and in community gatherings, food is an indispensable part of socializing and an important aspect of any festivity. To offer food to the guest is the duty and pleasure of the host and hostess, and to eat that food to the last morsel is the duty and delight of the guest. The ancient Hindu lawgiver Manu wrote: "Let not himself eat any delicate food without asking his guest to partake of it; the satisfaction of a guest will assuredly bring the housekeeper wealth, reputation, long life and a place in heaven." Food is given and accepted with an attitude of mutual appreciation. It establishes the concept of graceful give and take, and all other social interactions can be modeled upon it.

Throughout history, eating together has been the most basic form of community activity. It is the great equalizer. The dining table breaks down barriers faster than any bargaining table. When the great Sikh teacher Guru Amar Das was besieged by people wanting his advice, favor or arbitration, he devised a very clever way of setting an atmosphere of relaxation and equality among those seeking him out. In an age of prejudice and discrimination, he founded the langar or Guru's kitchen — the place where everyone, women and men, noblemen and peasants alike, had to first sit down side by side, without distinction, and be served a free meal. "First sit in a row in the kitchen, *then* seek the company of the Guru," he said. Wise politics: A tasty meal tends to enhance a sense of security and well-being and takes care of anxious butterflies in the stomach. It cools the temper and makes one feel that one has already been provided for regardless of one's query or complaint. Most important, one glance around the langar hall showed one that all people, no matter how dissimilar in appearance, how unequal in rank, how incompatible in emotion and intellectual bias, shared in the human condition — they all must eat to live, and everyone likes a good meal. The power of the cook in paving the path of peace should not be underestimated.

Perhaps the best way to bring the nations of the world into harmony would be to spread a dinner table that spans the globe. It would be a wonderful sight, all those different foods, cooked to perfection, with a rainbow of colors and a myriad of pleasing, tempting aromas, being shared in joy and gratitude by all the people of the world — and no reserved seating! Each one of us can start right now, in our own home, by trying the foods of other lands and by sharing the recipes and experience of other peoples to forge this eternal link of body and soul — the grace of God through the gift of food.

# Serving an Indian Meal

An Indian meal is a "mix and match" affair. All the foods, except for the appetizers and the dessert, are served at the same time. Vegetable main dishes, bean dishes, rice pilafs, yogurt salads, relishes, pickles and breads are all present in a magnificent display of color, aroma, texture and taste. Each member of the dinner party gets to choose the order in which his or her food shall be eaten, and "what gets combined with what." You eat a little bit of "samosa" . . . along with some hot "chutney," then try a taste with a sweet chutney, then a little bit of "subji" . . . and some "raita", then some rice with a saucy vegetable, then a piece of "chapati" and some "dahl" . . . and on and on in endless variety. Everyone participates in the art of culinary creation within his own plate!

At its simplest, an Indian meal consists of either a bean dish (dahl) or a vegetable dish (subji) and either rice or bread. A normal meal may include all of these, as well as yogurt or a yogurt dish (raita). At its most elaborate, an Indian meal will include two or more kinds of dahl, bread, rice, several vegetable dishes and chutneys, a dessert and a beverage. The more festive the occasion, the greater the number of dishes that are likely to be served.

The traditional way to serve an Indian meal is for each person to have a large, steep-sided metal plate called a "thali" on which are arranged several small metal bowls called "katoori". Each bowl is filled with a small portion of some vegetable dish, raita or dahl. Then on the large plate will also be heaped a portion of rice, as well as several servings of different kinds of chutneys and pickles. While the traditional plates and bowls are extremely practical, any

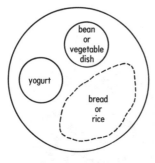

Simplest Meal

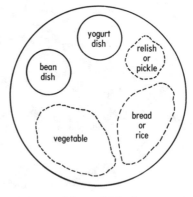

Normal Meal

comparable arrangement will do. The host or hostess usually spoons all of the courses onto each plate before serving it and, once everyone has been served, she checks frequently to see if anyone wants seconds.

A convenient alternative for many Western households is to serve family style or buffet style. Simply spread out all the different dishes in serving bowls and let everyone help themselves.

Appetizers are usually served informally before sitting down to dinner, often while the meal is still being prepared. Drinks such as "lassi" or fruit juice may be served as well. During the meal, the only liquid served is water. After everyone has eaten to complete satisfaction, the table is cleared and the sweet course brought in, sometimes with hot tea. And somehow, through the miracle of Indian cooking, everyone does manage just a little bit more!

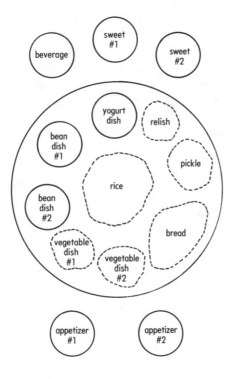

Very Festive Meal

# Helpful Hints for Food Preparation

Some of the ingredients in Indian cooking must be specially prepared before using. They are listed below. I've also shared some helpful hints about cooking and storing various foods.

*Almonds* can be peeled by putting them into a bowl and covering them with boiling water. After about 10 minutes pour off the water. You can then just "pinch" the skins right off. Or you can soak the almonds in water *overnight*, and by morning they will be ready to peel easily.

*Beans* have to be very carefully picked over before using. The simplest way to do this is to spread out the beans (or lentils or dried peas) in one layer on a cookie tray and sift through with your fingers and a sharp eye, looking for stones and debris. Very often the stone and bean look deceptively alike. After you've picked out all the stones, place the beans in a bowl, cover with water and swish the beans around. The dirt and debris will rise to the top of the water. Carefully pour off the water and wash once or twice until the water pours off clean.

*Cardamon pods* are useful primarily because of the little black seeds inside them. To get the seeds, crack open the pod with your fingernail and take out the seeds, discarding the pod. If you are de-seeding a lot of cardamon pods, spread them out in one layer on a clean surface and roll over them, pushing hard, with a rolling pin a few times. This will crack open the pods, and you can then remove the seeds.

*Chile powder* blends can be either mild or hot, according to preference. For hotter blends, add cayenne pepper to the normal mild chile powder blend.

*Cilantro* (coriander leaves) makes a nice addition to any Indian meal. Place finely chopped leaves in a bowl on the table as a do-it-yourself garnish.

*Coconuts* should be chosen free from cracks or mold. To open a coconut you can either pound around the "equator" of the coconut with a hammer until the shell cracks open — or you can "bake" it open. Just drill two holes in the "eyes" and drain out the milk. Then put the coconut in a 400 degree oven for 15-20 minutes. The shell will shrink. Take it out, hit it with a hammer and the shell should crack open. You can then peel away the brown inner skin with a sharp knife or vegetable peeler. Break into pieces and wash off any debris.

To grate the coconut, either cut it into little pieces and toss into an electric blender or food processor (with the metal blade), or hand grate it on the small holes of a metal grater. Extra fine grated coconut freezes very well (but freeze it in small batches, because once defrosted, it doesn't freeze well again).

*Deep frying* requires that the ghee or oil reaches its highest heat without burning, about 375 degrees, just before the smoking point. If it begins to smoke, turn down the heat. To test whether your oil is hot enough, stand back (oil splatters) and throw a sprinkle of water into the oil. It should crackle and pop wildly.

The important thing in deep frying is the freshness and flavor of the oil. For most deep fried foods, a bland oil such as sunflower or corn oil is best. After you've fried, let the oil cool down. Most of the debris from cooking will sink to the bottom of the pan. You can then pour off the top oil, straining it through several layers of cheesecloth into a jar, and store it for reuse in the refrigerator. If the oil has taken on the smell of the food you've just fried, you can re-use it for frying strong tasting foods like onions, garlic and ginger. Don't mix your oils or fry sweet delicate tasting food in oil that has been used for spicy foods. Deep frying with ghee is especially delicious, and the same method can be used to recover the leftover ghee. Refrigerate leftover ghee because it is no longer as pure as fresh ghee and can spoil.

*Freezing* Indian food is very simple. Most dishes with a gravy, "dry" vegetable dishes and bean dishes freeze very well. Rice, yogurt and sweet puddings lose their texture in freezing and are therefore not good choices for quantity cooking. In re-using frozen Indian food, the most important thing is to defrost properly. Take the food out of the freezer the night before and let it defrost completely before reheating. This way the texture stays the same and the delicate flavors can re-permeate the vegetables. Then place it in a saucepan and slowly heat it up. Herbs and spices lose much of their flavor in freezing, so you might want to perk up the reheated dish with some garam masala.

Most breads freeze well and can be reheated in the oven or the toaster oven. "Samosas" and "koftas" (vegetable balls) can be reheated by re-deep frying. Gulab Jamans, the sweet balls, can be frozen in plastic bags *without* having been cooked in their syrup. When needed, let them defrost, then cook them in a honey syrup for a few minutes before serving.

*Frying* flour, nuts, spices, onions, garlic, ginger, etc., demands your full attention. The chief thing to remember is that fried food turns into burnt food very suddenly. So stay alert and stir continually during the frying process.

To fry, start off with the oil warm rather than hot and let the ingredients and the oil then heat up to frying temperature together. This helps assure even frying. Hard spices such as mustard seeds, coriander seeds and fenugreek seeds take longer to fry than softer seeds such as cardamon or cumin, so start them off first. In frying onions, garlic and ginger, first fry the onions until they are almost done — limp, translucent and brown — *then* add the garlic and ginger, since they take much less time to brown. Because nuts contain so much oil, once they've given up their moisture, they tend to burn very quickly, so keep a vigilant eye on the frying pan.

*Garlic* should be felt carefully before buying to make sure there are no "empty feeling " spots — this indicates rotting or very old garlic that is shriveled up inside. To peel garlic easily, just break the bulb into cloves and place a clove under the flat side of a large kitchen knife. Press down firmly and "smash" the clove. The peel will break open and you can remove it easily.

If you've eaten a dish laced with garlic and are concerned about your breath, chew on a green cardamon pod (this also helps digestion), a clove or some fennel seeds.

*Ginger* is very knobby, with odd angles and protuberances. You can slice these odd pieces off and use them for making ginger tea, or you can carefully peel or scrape around them with a small sharp knife or a vegetable peeler. When you have a piece of ginger peeled, lay it on a cutting board and slice it very, very *thinly* with a sharp knife. You will find that each piece of ginger has a "grain," along which it slices easily. Then stack these slices in a pile and slice them again into long, thin, match-stick pieces. Gather these into a bundle and dice them into tiny bits. If not chopped carefully, your ginger may end up as a stringy lump rather than individual pieces.

*Green chiles* can be *hot*. They are sold fresh in most ethnic food stores and many supermarkets. They vary in size and length, but the ones traditionally used in Indian cooking are about 2-4 inches long and very thin. If not available, use Mexican Jalapeno or Serrano chiles (or mild green chiles, roasted so that skins can be removed, can be substituted if you prefer). The range of hotness varies considerably, so try a bit of each chile before you use it to determine how much you really want in that recipe. Experienced cooks can tell the hotness just by breaking a chile and smelling it, and with a little experience you can too. The wide stem end of the chile is hotter than the narrow tip, and the core and seeds inside are the hottest parts. For the timid, therefore, it is best to remove the insides and use only the outsides for cooking. To remove the insides, cut off the stem end, slice the chile in half lengthwise and scrape out the core and the seeds.

Just by handling a green chile you may experience a burning sensation on your hands. Use plastic gloves if you have sensitive skin or if you are going to handle a baby afterwards. Be sure not to touch your face, especially your eyes, until you've washed your hands thoroughly with soap and water. The burning is caused by an acid in the chile. If necessary, use milk or baking soda to neutralize it.

*Pressure cooking* saves time, improves food flavor and color, preserves vitamins and minerals, and lowers cooking fuel costs. As such, it is a worthwhile addition to any serious cook's kitchen. It is particularly useful in Indian cooking as a means of cutting in half the cooking time for bean (dahl) dishes, which are traditionally served with meals, and is also useful in cooking vegetables.

The best kind of pressure cooker is stainless steel, which does not react with foods being cooked. The instruction booklet that comes with your pressure cooker should indicate modifications of cooking time and quantities (such as amount of water to be added) when cooking with the pressure cooker.

*Rice*, when purchased in bulk food stores, is often full of debris such as bits of vegetable matter, dirt or pebbles. First, stones should be picked out carefully. Then wash the rice by placing it in a large bowl and running cool water over it. Swish the rice around with your hands. The debris and a whitish powder will rise to the top of the water. Carefully pour off the water and repeat the washing process two or three times until the water turns clear.

*Roasting* spices, nuts or flour requires even more vigilance than frying. To roast, first heat your thick-bottomed frying pan, then add the spices or nuts, shaking the pan continuously. The spices or nuts are done when they are deep brown but not burnt. Spices can then be ground with a mortar and pestle or in an electric coffee grinder or blender. Store ground spices in an airtight container away from the light.

# The Basic Recipes

Fragrant and enticing, traditional Indian cooking relies heavily upon a few basic recipes: garam masala, ghee, chenna, panir, khoa and yogurt. They form the foundation upon which the temple of Indian cuisine is built. Any one of them may be used in the preparation of several dishes within the same meal. The ghee prepared for stuffed prantha is used in Bengali Style Potatoes and Cabbage as well as sweet "laddu"; the cubes of panir are equally delicious soaking up the pistachio cream of "rasmalai" or swimming in the tangy tomato sauce of Matar Panir. Once they become an easy part of your repertoire, then delicious, authentic meals can be easily prepared.

# Khoa - Unsweetened Condensed Milk
## (Khoaa)

Khoa, made from whole milk, is the creamy, fudge-like base of many exquisite Indian candies and sweets. It takes a fairly long time to make (the milk cooks down slowly to about one quarter of its volume), but it really is the only way to get that incredible light creaminess which makes "barfi" such a special treat.

*1/2 gallon milk*

Note: Making khoa is time-consuming but well worth the effort. There is no substitute for the taste. Four parts milk converts into approximately one part khoa. If, however, you are very pressed for time, substitute canned (unsweetened) evaporated milk for khoa.

In a large, thick-bottomed saucepan, heat the milk to boiling, *stirring continuously* to prevent sticking. Keep boiling and stirring vigorously until the moisture is evaporated from the milk and a smooth, very thick cream is formed. Remove from the heat and let cool. Store in a covered container in the refrigerator.

Yield: 2½ cups khoa

# Chenna and Panir - Soft Creamy Cheese

Panir *(paneer)* is *the* Indian cheese, similar to Italian ricotta cheese but much drier. Made from split milk, in the rough curd form it is called chenna, and when it is compressed and cut into cubes it is called panir. It is used in all aspects of Indian cookery: appetizers, main dishes and desserts.

*1/2 gallon milk*
*1/4 cup lemon juice or 3*
*teaspoons cream of tartar*
*plus 1 cup hot water*

1) In a large, thick-bottomed saucepan, heat the milk to the boiling point, stirring frequently to avoid sticking. Then remove from the heat. Immediately and little by little, add the lemon juice or add cream of tartar dissolved in hot water, stirring gently. When the milk splits into lumpy, white curds and a watery, greenish whey, stop adding lemon juice or cream of tartar. Cover and let stand for 15 minutes.

Note: If too much lemon juice or cream of tartar is added, the panir will be suspended in the whey in fine particles which will be very difficult to separate out.

2) Line a colander with several layers of cheesecloth. Place the colander in the sink, or a basin if you intend to keep the whey. Pour the curdled milk into the colander. The cheesecloth will let the whey drain through and trap the curds.

3) When all the liquid is drained off, wrap the cheesecloth tightly around the curds and hang this "bag" of curds over the sink or a basin to let any remaining liquid drip off from the curds. The curds, once they have been drained, are called chenna (*chainaa*).

4) When no more moisture is dripping off, place the wrapped curds in a baking dish, placing a heavy weight on top of the curds, and keep this set-up in the refrigerator overnight. This will form the curds into a solid mass of cheese. In the morning this cheese can be unwrapped and cut into cubes or molded into balls.

Note: Panir will keep fresh in the refrigerator for 3 or 4 days. The whey is a healthful drink; children love it mixed half and half with apple juice.

Yield: 1¼ cups (¾ pound) panir (cheese) and over 1 quart whey

# Ghee · Clarified Butter

Ghee is butter that is allowed to simmer for a long time so the moisture from the milk solids evaporates completely. Meanwhile, the impurities in the butter sink to the bottom of the pan as a discardable residue. Ghee has a wonderful, slightly nutty flavor and is very low in cholesterol.

*9 pounds unsalted butter*

Note: Ghee keeps without refrigeration for 3-4 months when stored in a closed container, up to 1 year in the refrigerator, and nearly forever frozen. Therefore, since it is time-consuming to make, it pays to make a large quantity at a time. Once you start using ghee instead of oil for frying and in place of butter on toast, you won't want to use anything else.

One pound of unsalted butter will yield approximately 1½ cups of ghee.

To make ghee you will need a 12-quart, stainless steel, thick-bottomed saucepan. (In the process the ghee foams up, so you will need to leave plenty of room in your pan.)

1) Slowly heat the butter until completely melted, then raise the heat to high and continue cooking, stirring often. Take care to frequently scrape the bottom of the pot. The butter will come to a foaming boil, and the heat may need to be reduced until the foam subsides to keep it from boiling over.

2) After about 12-15 minutes of boiling, the butter oil (ghee) will start to show a separation from the milk solids. The oil is translucent yellow, and the milk solids are thick and white. Continue cooking and stirring.

3) After another 5-8 minutes, the oil will separate out more, becoming almost clear, and the solids will disintegrate into small particles with a slightly reddish-orange tinge, indicating the ghee is done. The smell is delicious. Remove the pot from the stove to a safe place, where it will not be disturbed as it cools. When the ghee

is properly cooked, all of the milk solids will settle to the bottom of the pot.

4) After several hours, carefully pour off all of the ghee into a clean, wide-mouthed glass gallon jar through several layers of cheesecloth (held onto the jar with rubber bands). Store at room temperature with the jar covered. Discard the milk solids. Ghee will keep indefinitely without refrigeration, and it has all the flavor of butter with fewer calories and no saturated fat.

# Ghee — Slow Cooker Method

*4 pounds unsalted butter*

Place the butter in a 6-quart slow cooker. Let cook at medium heat for 12 hours, then . . . ghee! Just pour off the oil as described in above recipe and store in a glass jar.

# Garam Masala - Spice Mixture
## *(Garam masaalaa)*

Garam Masala is a blend (masala) of warm or hot (garam) spices. These terms "warm" or "hot" do not refer to the "spiciness" on the palate, but to the medicinal properties of the spice. Warm or hot spices are those that help generate body heat and are therefore good to eat in cold weather. Bay leaf, black cardamon, cinnamon, ginger, mace, nutmeg and red pepper are examples. Cool spices are those that take heat away from your system: fennel, cloves and green cardamon are some of these cooling spices.

There are many different blends of garam masala. As you become more familiar with the recipes in this book and sensitive to your own subtle taste preferences, you might find yourself varying these basic garam masala recipes a bit to suit your own needs. Imported garam masala can be purchased in tins or boxes in Indian specialty food stores and even some supermarkets, but they are sometimes stale from the long periods of shipping and storage. Since so much of Indian food's special taste and aroma comes from the spices, it really pays to make your own garam masala.

| | |
|---|---|
| 1 cup coriander seeds | 1 1/2 cinnamon sticks |
| 1/2 cup cumin seeds | 1/2 cup black peppercorns |
| 1/2 cup black cardamon pods | 1/4 cup whole cloves |
| (use only the seeds) | 1 teaspoon nutmeg powder |

In an electric blender, coffee grinder or spice mill, grind the spices to a fine powder. Store in an airtight container.

## Special Masala - Special Spice Blend

There are as many kinds of masala as there are cooks in India. Here is my "Special Masala" which you can use in some other recipes later on in this book.

| | |
|---|---|
| 1 teaspoon powdered black | 1/2 teaspoon salt |
| pepper | 1 teaspoon cumin powder |
| 1 teaspoon red chile powder | 3 teaspoons mango powder |

Mix all the spices together. Store in an airtight container.

## Yogurt
### (Dahee)

Yogurt, whether served plain or with vegetables and seasonings, is a part of most Indian meals. Although store-bought yogurt can be used, for real authentic taste and consistency, and for maximum health benefits, homemade yogurt is best. Here's how to make it:

| | |
|---|---|
| 1 quart milk | 2-3 tablespoons yogurt |

Pour milk into a saucepan. Heat it slowly so as not to scorch it. Just short of boiling, remove it from the heat and let it cool to a lukewarm temperature, about 118 degrees F. As it cools, stir it occasionally. Then add 2 to 3 tablespoons of already made yogurt as a "starter" and stir gently and thoroughly. You can leave the milk in the saucepan, covered, or you can pour it into a sterilized jar with a lid. Wrap tightly in a towel to hold in the heat, and place in a warm, dark place where the temperature can be maintained for 6 to 7 hours. A gas oven with only the pilot light on works well. An insulated cooler or a cardboard carton covered with a blanket can also be used. Let it sit undisturbed. The temperature must be neither too hot nor too cold, or the yogurt won't form. After 6 to 7 hours, you can remove it from its "hiding place" and refrigerate.

# Snacks and Appetizers

Formally, the Indian meal consists of only the main course followed by the sweet course. However, it is quite common for Indian families to serve a beginning course of snacks or appetizers while everyone is waiting for dinner to be served, especially when guests have been invited.

Salty or savory snacks *(chat)* are, for the most part, deep-fried finger foods or rich, filled pastries. When serving these as an opening to a meal, go easy. These foods are very rich and extremely delicious. The tendency to fill up on appetizers can blunt the comfortable enjoyment of the rest of the meal.

Outside of dinner hours whenever a visitor arrives, snacks are served, usually with hot or cold drinks, depending on the season. It's considered the most basic form of hospitality, deeply rooted in Indian tradition. Since snacks are served so often, and since they must be ready at a moment's notice, the culture of India has developed a great variety of easy-to-make snack items that either store well or can be whipped up fresh at a moment's notice. These are often served with a choice of tangy or sweet chutneys for dipping. When necessary, snacks can serve as a very tasty light meal.

Many of the filled pastries and balls can be made in quantity, frozen and then deep fried as needed. The biscuits and crackers will keep fresh for a long time when stored in an airtight container.

Snack time in India includes both sweet and salty snacks served right alongside each other. The recipes for the sweet snacks can be found in the chapter on sweets and desserts.

*Cutlets and Kabobs:*

These can be served for breakfast or as a snack, with evening tea, as a cocktail, or a colorful dish at dinner.

# Deep Fried Cashew Cutlets
## (Kaajoo Tikkee)

For the cutlets:

1 teaspoon ghee

4 teaspoons unbleached white flour

4 green chiles, hot or mild, to taste, seeded

1½ cups milk

2 cups fresh bread crumbs or 1 cup Matzo Meal (Manischewitz)

1 cup cashews, chopped coarsely

¼ cup fresh coriander leaves

---

3 teaspoons tomato sauce

¼ teaspoon white pepper powder

½ teaspoon mustard powder

½ teaspoon salt, or to taste

---

For the batter:

½ cup unbleached white flour

½ cup water

½ cup fine dry bread crumbs for dusting

---

2 cups vegetable oil or ghee for deep frying

1 tomato, wedged

---

For the decoration:

a few lettuce leaves

1 radish, sliced thinly

1) In a large, thick-bottomed frying pan or wok, heat the ghee and saute the 4 teaspoons of unbleached white flour and the green chiles until the flour is slightly browned. Add the milk and cook until thickened, *stirring continuously.* Then add the fresh bread crumbs, cashews and coriander leaves. Continue to cook, *stirring continuously* until very thick. Then remove from the heat.

2) Add the tomato sauce, white pepper, mustard and salt, mixing thoroughly. Spread this mixture in a cookie tray and press it down flat. Place it in the freezer for 15 minutes, until it becomes firm.

3) In a bowl, mix a ½ cup of unbleached white flour with enough water to form a batter (about ½ cup).

4) Remove the cashew spread from the freezer and cut out cutlets with a heart shaped cookie cutter. Dip each one in the batter, then coat it completely with fine bread crumbs.

5) In a thick-bottomed saucepan, heat the vegetable oil or ghee until ready. (See "Deep Frying," p. 19.) Carefully immerse the cutlets in the hot oil and deep fry until golden brown. Remove with a slotted spoon, letting the excess oil drip back into the pan. Drain further on paper towels.

6) Serve the cutlets arranged on a bed of cooked basmati rice and garnish with lettuce, radish and tomato. Serve with mint or tomato chutney. Served alone they make a high-protein breakfast food.

Yield: 16 cutlets

# Deep Fried Vegetable Rice Cutlets
## (Sabjee Chaawal Tikkee)

A crispy main dish with a mild flavor.

For the cutlets:

2¼ cups milk

5 green chiles, mild or hot, to taste, chopped

3 tablespoons ghee

---

⅓ cup or more rice powder

2 small carrots, diced and steamed

½ cup green peas, cooked

a few coriander leaves

½ teaspoon salt, or to taste

½ teaspoon mustard powder

3 teaspoons tomato sauce

---

For the batter:

1 cup unbleached white flour

1 cup water

---

1 cup fine dry bread crumbs for dusting

2-3 cups vegetable oil or ghee for deep frying

---

For decoration:

1 boiled beet

1 tomato

1 cucumber

2-3 lettuce leaves

1) In a thick-bottomed saucepan, boil the milk with the green chiles and 3 tablespoons of ghee. Stir in the rice powder and cook it, stirring continuously until it becomes quite thick. (Add a little more rice powder, if necessary, to thicken.) Add the carrots and peas. Remove from the heat. Mix in the coriander leaves, salt, mustard and tomato sauce. Stir thoroughly.

2) Spread this mixture out on a cookie sheet and refrigerate until it is solid. Then remove from the refrigerator and cut into cutlets with a large cookie cutter.

3) In a bowl, make a batter out of the unbleached white flour and water. Dip the cutlets into the batter, then into the bread crumbs.

4) In a thick-bottomed saucepan, heat the 2-3 cups of vegetable oil or ghee for deep frying. Carefully immerse the cutlets in the oil and deep fry until golden brown. Remove with a slotted spoon, letting

the excess oil drip back into the pan. Drain further on paper towels.

5) Serve piping hot, arranged on a platter and decorate with sliced, colorful vegetables such as beet, tomato, cucumber, lettuce leaves.

Yield: about 20 cutlets

# Corn Fritters
## *(Makee Vadaa)*

| | |
|---|---|
| *1 cup maize (dried whole corn kernels)* | *3 cups hot water* |

| | |
|---|---|
| *1 medium onion, chopped* | *1 teaspoon ground black* |
| *2 tablespoons lime juice* | *pepper* |
| *2 tablespoons green chiles, mild or hot to taste, chopped* | *½ teaspoon salt, or to taste* |
| *2 teaspoons cumin seeds* | *1 tablespoon unbleached white flour* |

*2 cups vegetable oil or ghee for deep frying*

1) Immerse the corn in hot water and let soak *overnight*.

2) Drain the water off the corn. Grind in the blender onion first, then add lime juice, corn, chiles, cumin, black pepper, salt and flour and blend until a thick paste is formed.

3) With this paste form small balls, about the size of a walnut, then flatten them out into a thick patty.

4) In a thick-bottomed saucepan or wok, heat the vegetable oil or ghee to the smoking point. Immerse the patties in the hot oil and deep fry until golden brown. Remove with a slotted spoon, letting the excess oil drip back into the pan. Drain further on paper towels. Serve hot.

Yield: 20 fritters

# Deep Fried Cream of Wheat Cutlets
## (Soojee Tikkee)

For the cutlets:

1 cup milk

2 tablespoons sweet butter

2¼ cups cream of wheat

---

2 green chiles mild or hot, to taste, chopped fine

½ teaspoon crushed dry red chiles

½ teaspoon finely chopped peeled fresh ginger

1½ teaspoons fresh coriander leaves, chopped

1 teaspoon salt, or to taste

1½ teaspoons tomato sauce

---

For the batter:

½ cup unbleached white flour

½ cup water

---

½ cup fine dry bread crumbs for dusting

2 cups vegetable oil or ghee for deep frying

1) In a thick-bottomed saucepan heat the milk and butter together, then add the cream of wheat. Cook on a low heat, stirring continuously, until the oil starts to separate out. Then add the green chiles, crushed red chiles, ginger, coriander leaves, salt and tomato sauce, stirring well.

2) Spread the mixture on a cookie sheet and refrigerate until it hardens. Then remove from the refrigerator and cut into simple cutlet shapes with a cookie cutter.

3) In a bowl, make a thin batter of unbleached white flour and water. Carefully dip the cutlets into this batter and then into the bread crumbs.

4) In a thick-bottomed saucepan, heat the vegetable oil or ghee for deep frying. Carefully immerse the cutlets in the hot oil and deep fry until golden brown. Remove with a slotted spoon, letting the excess oil drip back into the pan. Drain further on paper towels.

Yield: 9-10 cutlets

# Potato Cream Rolls
## (Makhnee Aaloo Tikkee)

For the potato rolls:

2 medium potatoes

1 teaspoon salt

---

1 teaspoon butter

½ teaspoon crushed dry red chiles

3 green chiles, mild or hot, to taste, chopped fine

2 teaspoons peeled, finely chopped, fresh ginger

a few fresh coriander leaves, chopped

½ teaspoon salt, or to taste

¼ cup cream

---

For the batter:

2 tablespoons unbleached white flour

2 tablespoons water

---

2 tablespoons fine bread-crumbs for dusting

2 cups vegetable oil or ghee for deep frying

1) Boil the potatoes until tender in water with 1 teaspoon of salt added to it. Remove the potatoes from the water and set aside to cool. Then peel and grate them.

2) In a large, thick-bottomed frying pan, heat the butter and add the red and green chiles, chopped ginger, coriander leaves and ½ teaspoon salt. Mix in the grated potatoes and cook for 1 minute. Add the cream, mix well and set aside.

3) Make a thin batter of the flour and water. Flour your hands, take a handful of the potato mixture and form into a roll. Dip this roll in the batter, then dust it with the bread crumbs.

4) In a thick-bottomed saucepan or wok, heat the vegetable oil or ghee for deep frying. Carefully slip the rolls into the hot oil and deep fry on a low heat until brown. Remove with a slotted spoon, letting the excess oil drip back into the pan. Drain further on paper towels. Serve hot.

Yield: 24 potato rolls

# Coconut-Raisin Potato Kabobs
## (Aaloo Kabaab)

A delightful and unusual appetizer.

For the kabobs:

| | |
|---|---|
| 2 large potatoes | 2 teaspoons salt |

| | |
|---|---|
| 2 tablespoons ghee (for stuffing) | 1 small tomato, chopped |
| 1½ cups fresh coconut, grated | 1 tablespoon raisins |
| 1 teaspoon fresh ginger, peeled and finely chopped | 1 teaspoon salt, or to taste |
| 1 tablespoon fresh coriander leaves, chopped | 2 slices toasted or dry bread, crust removed, crumbled |
| 2 green chiles, mild or hot, to taste, chopped fine | 1 teaspoon white cumin powder |
| | ½ teaspoon garam masala |

For the batter:

| | |
|---|---|
| ½ cup unbleached white flour | 1 cup water |

1 cup fine bread crumbs

2 cups vegetable oil or ghee
for deep frying

1) Boil the potatoes in water with 2 teaspoons of salt added to it. When tender, remove from water, let cool, then peel (if desired) and grate.

2) In a thick-bottomed frying pan or wok, melt the two tablespoons of ghee and add the fresh coconut, ginger root, coriander, green chiles, tomato and raisins. Add 1 teaspoon salt, crumbled bread, cumin and garam masala. Mix it all together and fry for a few minutes. Then add the grated potatoes, mix well and set aside.

3) Make a thick batter of the flour and water. Flour your hands, take a small handful of the potato mixture and form into an oblong roll about 2 inches long. Dip the roll in the batter, then coat it with the bread crumbs.

4) In a thick-bottomed saucepan or wok, heat the 2 cups of vegetable oil or ghee for deep frying. Carefully slip the potato rolls into the hot oil and deep fry until golden brown. Remove with a slotted spoon, letting the excess oil drip back into the pan. Further drain on paper towels. Serve hot with mint chutney.

Yield: 20-25 2-inch-long kabobs

# Crisp Potato Balls
## (Aaloo Kabaab)

| | |
|---|---|
| 1/3 cup small or instant tapioca | 2 cups water |

| | |
|---|---|
| 2 medium potatoes | 1/2 cup fresh coriander leaves, |
| 5 green chiles, mild or hot, to | chopped |
| taste, chopped fine | 1 teaspoon salt, or to taste |

1/2 cup garbanzo flour

2 cups vegetable oil or ghee
  for deep frying

1) Soak the tapioca in water *overnight* . Then strain off the water and squeeze the tapioca with your hands to remove any remaining liquid.

2) Boil the potatoes until tender. Remove from the water and, if desired, peel. Mash the potatoes together with the tapioca. Mix in the chopped green chiles, coriander leaves and salt. Form this mixture into balls, about 1/2 inch in diameter. Roll each ball in the garbanzo flour, coating it completely.

3) In a thick-bottomed saucepan, heat the vegetable oil or ghee for deep frying. Carefully immerse the balls in the hot oil, a few at a time, and deep fry until golden brown. Remove with a slotted spoon, letting the excess oil drip back into the pan. Drain further on paper towels. Serve hot with chutney.

Yield: 50 potato balls

# Spicy Rich Vegetable Kabobs
## (Sabjee Kabaab)

For the kabobs:
1 ½ pounds root vegetables
    or potatoes (equivalent to 2
    large potatoes)

---

4 green cardamon pods (use
    only the seeds)
1 small onion, chopped fine
6 almonds, chopped fine
5 green chiles, mild or hot, to
    taste, chopped fine

1 teaspoon fresh ginger,
    peeled and finely chopped
2 teaspoons cumin powder
1 teaspoon garam masala
¼ teaspoon red chile powder
1 teaspoon salt, or to taste

---

3 tablespoons vegetable oil or
    ghee

¼ cup garbanzo flour

---

For the dip:
½ cup yogurt

¼-⅓ cup fresh mint leaves,
    chopped fine

---

For the batter:
½-1 cup unbleached white
    flour

⅓-⅞ cup water

---

1 cup fine bread crumbs for dusting
2 cups vegetable oil or ghee for deep frying

1) Peel and cut the root vegetables or potatoes into small pieces and steam until tender. Set aside to cool.

2) Remove the seeds from the green cardamon pods and crush them with a rolling pin. Mix together the cardamon, onion, almonds, green chiles, ginger, cumin, garam masala, red chile and salt. Mash the roots or potatoes, then add the spice mixture and mix thoroughly.

3) In a large, thick-bottomed frying pan, heat the 3 tablespoons of vegetable oil or ghee and saute the garbanzo flour until light brown. Add this to the root or potato mixture and mix well.

4) In a separate bowl prepare the yogurt dip:

Place the yogurt in the center of a piece of cheesecloth. Gather the corners together and hang it up above a sink or basin so the water can drain off the yogurt.

When all the liquid has dripped off, mix this thick yogurt together with the mint leaves. Set aside.

5) In another bowl, mix the unbleached white flour with enough water to form a batter the consistency of thick pancake batter. Set aside.

6) Take small handfuls of the root or potato mixture and form into small, oblong rolls with your hands. First dip each roll into the yogurt mixture, coating it completely. Then dip it into the batter. And finally, dust it with the bread crumbs.

7) In a thick-bottomed saucepan or wok, heat the vegetable oil or ghee for deep frying. Carefully slip the rolls into the hot oil and deep fry on a low heat until brown. Remove with a slotted spoon, letting the excess oil drip back into the pan. Drain further on paper towels. Serve hot.

Yield: about 2 dozen kabobs

*Stuffed Pastry and Biscuits*

# Vegetable Patties
## *(Saamosaa)*

Good for a formal breakfast, samosas can be made in quantity, kept frozen and then heated in the oven at 350 degrees for a fancy treat on short notice. When hot they will taste freshly baked.

For the pastry:

2 cups unbleached white flour
2 teaspoons salt
4 teaspoons melted ghee or
  vegetable oil for pastry

16-20 tablespoons water

---

For the filling:

4 medium potatoes
3 tablespoons melted ghee or
  vegetable oil for filling
3 teaspoons coriander powder
3 teaspoons cumin powder
1 teaspoon crushed dry red
  chiles
6 green chiles, mild or hot, to
  taste, chopped fine

1/2 teaspoon ground black
  pepper
1 teaspoon fresh coriander
  leaves, chopped
2 tablespoons dry pome-
  granate seeds
1 teaspoon salt, or to taste
1/4 cup green peas, fresh or
  frozen

---

2 cups vegetable oil or ghee
  for deep frying

*To make the pastry:*
1) In a bowl, sift together the flour and 2 teaspoons of salt. Add the 4 teaspoons of ghee, working it into the flour with your fingertips. Make a well in the center of the flour and slowly add the water, gradually mixing in the flour to form a soft dough. Knead for a few minutes.

2) Break off a piece of dough and form into a ball about the size of a walnut. On a lightly floured pastry board or flat surface, roll out the ball with a rolling pin to form a thin, round pancake.

3) Cut this pancake in half and fit the two half-circles thus formed on top of each other. With a fork, press together the round edge, leaving the straight edge open. Keep a damp cloth over the pastry so it doesn't dry out.

*To make the filling:*
1) Boil the potatoes until tender. Then peel them and dice into small cubes.

2) In a large, thick-bottomed frying pan or wok, heat the vegetable oil or ghee and add the coriander powder, cumin, red chiles, green chiles, black pepper, coriander leaves, pomegranate seeds and 1 teaspoon of salt, along with the potatoes and peas. Mix thoroughly and cook on a low heat for 2 minutes, stirring continuously. Then set aside to cool.

*To make the turnovers:*
1) Stuff the half-circle pastry pocket with the potato-pea filling. Seal the straight edge by moistening it with a little water and pinching it closed.

2) In a deep, thick-bottomed saucepan, heat the 2 cups of vegetable oil or ghee. (See "Deep Frying," p. 19.) Then turn down the heat. Carefully immerse the turnovers in the hot oil and deep fry on a low heat until golden brown. Remove from the oil with a slotted spoon, letting the excess oil drip back into the pan. Drain further on paper towels.

3) Serve hot with chutney or ketchup.

Yield: 16-20 patties

# Deep Fried Bean-Filled Pancake
## (Khastaa Kachoree)

Serve as a snack or for breakfast.

For the beans:
½ cup urad dahl (split black mung beans)

1½ cups water for soaking

For the pastry:
1 cup whole wheat pastry flour
½ teaspoon salt
2 teaspoons vegetable oil for pastry

2 tablespoons ghee for pastry
¾ cup lukewarm water

For the filling:
2 tablespoons ghee for filling
1 teaspoon red chile powder
3 teaspoons coriander powder

1 teaspoon black cumin seeds
¼ teaspoon baking soda
2 teaspoons water

2 cups vegetable oil or ghee for deep frying

Soak the well-washed beans in 1½ cups of water *overnight*. Then cook them on a medium heat for *2 hours,* or until soft.

*To make the pastry:*
1) In a bowl, sift together the flour and salt. Add the 2 teaspoons of oil and the 2 tablespoons of ghee, working them into the flour with your fingertips. Gradually add the ¾ cup of lukewarm water until a lump of dough is formed.

2) Place the dough on a lightly floured pastry board or flat surface and knead for 5 minutes, until smooth and pliable. Break off a small piece of dough and form into a ball approximately 1½ inches in diameter. (Cover the balls with a damp cloth to keep them from drying out.)

44

*To make the filling:*
In a thick-bottomed frying pan, heat the 2 tablespoons of ghee and saute the chile powder, coriander, cumin, baking soda and the 2 teaspoons of water until brown. Then mix in the cooked dahl and stir thoroughly. Remove from the heat and cool.

*To make the filled pancakes:*
1) Lightly dust a pastry board or flat surface with ¼ cup of flour as needed. Using a rolling pin, roll the dough ball out halfway. Place a portion of the filling in the center, then fold the sides of the dough up over the filling. Using your hands, carefully press the filled ball out into a pancake about 3 inches in diameter.

2) In a thick-bottomed saucepan, heat the 2 cups of vegetable oil or ghee to smoking point, then turn down to a medium heat. Carefully immerse the pancakes in the hot oil and deep fry until golden brown. Remove with a slotted spoon, letting the excess oil drip back into the pan. Drain further on paper towels. Serve hot.

Yield: 12 stuffed pancakes

# Punjabi-Style Bean-Filled Pancake
## *(Punjaabee Kachoree)*

For breakfast, snack or special luncheon

For the beans:
*½ cup pink lentils (masur ki dahl)*          *1½ cups water for soaking*

---

For the pastry:
*1 cup unbleached white flour*          *⅓ cup warm water*
*½ teaspoon salt*          *3 teaspoons yogurt*
*¼ cup ghee or vegetable oil*

---

For the filling:
*¼ teaspoon baking soda*          *2 teaspoons red chile powder*
*½ teaspoon salt*          *2 teaspoons coriander powder*
*2 teaspoons black cumin powder*          *2 tablespoons ghee*
          *2 teaspoons cream of wheat*

---

For the pancakes:
*¼ cup of flour for dusting*          *2 cups vegetable oil or ghee for deep frying*

*To prepare the beans:*
Soak the well washed pink lentils in 1½ cups water for 3-4 hours.

*To make the pastry:*
1)In a bowl, sift together the cup of flour and the ½ teaspoon of salt. Add the ¼ cup of ghee or vegetable oil, working it into the flour with your fingertips. Add the warm water and yogurt and mix until a compact mass of dough is formed.

2) On a lightly floured pastry board or flat surface, knead the dough for 5 minutes until soft, smooth and pliable.

3) Break off a piece of dough and form into a ball about 1½ inches in diameter. (Cover the balls with a damp cloth to keep them from drying out.)

46

*To make the filling:*
Drain the water off the soaked pink lentils. Add the baking soda, ½ teaspoon of salt, cumin, chile and coriander. In a thick-bottomed frying pan, heat the 2 tablespoons of ghee and saute the lentil-spice mixture on a low heat for 5 minutes. Add the cream of wheat, mix thoroughly, and continue to saute until light brown. Set aside to cool.

*To make the filled pancakes:*
1) Lightly dust a pastry board or flat surface with ¼ cup of flour, as needed. Using a rolling pin, roll the dough ball out halfway. Place a portion of the filling in the center, then fold the sides of the dough up, over the filling. Using your hands, carefully press the filled ball into a pancake about 3 inches in diameter.

2) In a thick-bottomed saucepan, heat the vegetable oil or ghee to smoking point, then turn down to a medium heat. Carefully immerse the pancakes in the hot oil and deep fry until golden brown. Remove with a slotted spoon, letting the excess oil drip back into the pan. Drain further on paper towels. Serve hot.

Yield: 12 stuffed pancakes

# Curried Cheese Cubes
## (Masaalaa Paneer)

*1 cup panir (see recipe p. 24)*

---

*⅛ teaspoon ground red chile
  (mild)*
*⅛ teaspoon turmeric*
*1 tablespoon ginger powder
  (blended with 1 tablespoon
  water)*

*2 teaspoons mango powder
  (or lemon juice)*
*½ teaspoon salt, or to taste*

---

*2 teaspoons garbanzo flour*

---

*2 cups vegetable oil or ghee
  for deep frying*

1) Prepare the panir according to the recipe on p. 24 and cut into cubes.

2) Mix together the red chile, turmeric, ginger/water, mango powder (or lemon juice) and salt, and sprinkle over the panir cubes until each cube is well coated.

3) Lightly dust each cube with garbanzo flour.

4) In a thick-bottomed saucepan or wok, heat the vegetable oil or ghee to the smoking point, then carefully immerse the panir cubes into the oil, deep frying until brown. Remove with a slotted spoon, letting the excess oil drip back into the pan. Drain further on paper towels. Serve hot, with chutney or hot sauce.

Yield: 15 1-inch-square cubes

# Party Wafers
## (Golgappa)

These wafers are a flaky appetizer or side dish. Serve with "Jaljeera" (p. 157).

| | |
|---|---|
| ¾ cup whole wheat pastry flour | 4 teaspoons cream of wheat |
| | ½ cup of water |

| | |
|---|---|
| ¼ cup flour for dusting pastry board | 2 cups vegetable oil or ghee for deep frying |

1) In a bowl, mix together the whole wheat pastry flour and the cream of wheat. Gradually add the water, mixing to form a lump of dough. Knead the dough until soft and pliable. (Time and effort may be saved by kneading the dough with a suitably equipped food processor.)

2) Place the dough on a lightly floured (from the ¼ cup) pastry board or flat surface and roll it out into a long, thin loaf with your hands. Cut off small pieces, about the size of an almond, and form these, either with your hands or with a rolling pin, into small, thin, disk-shaped rounds. Cover them with a damp cloth to keep them from drying out.

3) In a thick-bottomed saucepan, heat the vegetable oil or ghee to smoking point and deep fry the pastry rounds 3 or 4 at a time. They will puff up and pop to the surface while frying. They cook quickly. Scoop out with a slotted spoon, letting the excess oil drip back into the pan.

4) These wafers (golgappas) are served by making a small hole in the side and filling with a couple of cooked chickpeas then pouring jaljeera (see recipe, p. 157) into the hole. Those rounds that do not puff up are called paparies and are equally delicious.

Yield: 32 wafers

# Deep Fried Biscuit
## *(Mathee)*

A really scrumptious snack at home or for the road. Good eaten hot with jam.

1 cup unbleached white flour
1 teaspoon salt
½ teaspoon oregano seeds
3 tablespoons melted ghee or
   butter

6 tablespoons water
¼ cup flour for dusting pastry
   board
2 cups vegetable oil or ghee
   for deep frying

1) In a bowl, sift together the flour and salt. Add the oregano seeds and mix thoroughly. Then add the melted ghee or butter, working it into the flour with your fingertips until the flour is like dry crumbs. Gradually add the water, mixing until a fairly stiff dough is formed.

2) Place the dough on a lightly floured pastry board or flat surface and knead for 5 minutes. Then break off a small piece of dough the size of an almond. With a rolling pin, roll these pieces out into little disks a little thicker than a chapati. These disks (some of which might be actually triangular in shape) will be cracked around the edges.

3) In a thick-bottomed saucepan, heat the vegetable oil or ghee to smoking point, then turn down the heat. Immerse the disks in the hot oil a few at a time and deep fry, turning frequently, until golden brown. Remove with a slotted spoon, letting the excess oil drip back into the pan. Drain further on paper towels. Stored in an airtight container, these biscuits will keep for 8-10 weeks.

Yield: 12-16 3-inch-wide biscuits

# Punjabi Style Deep Fried Biscuit
## (Punjaabee Mathee)

For breakfast, a take-along snack, or with tea or coffee. Rich and spicy.

1 cup unbleached white flour
1 teaspoon black peppercorns,
   crushed
1/2 teaspoon oregano seeds
1 teaspoon salt

1/4 teaspoon baking soda
1/4 cup ghee
1/2 cup water
2 teaspoons yogurt

---

1/4 cup flour for dusting pastry
   board

---

2 cups vegetable oil or ghee
   for deep frying

1) Sift the flour into a bowl. Add the crushed black peppercorns, oregano seeds, salt and baking soda and mix well. Melt the ghee and work into the flour with your fingertips. Then add the water and yogurt and mix thoroughly, forming a stiff dough.

2) Place the dough on a lightly floured (1/4 cup, as needed) pastry board or flat surface and knead for a few minutes. Break off small pieces of dough to form small balls. With a rolling pin, roll the dough ball out into thick biscuits, approximately 2 inches in diameter.

3) In a thick-bottomed saucepan, heat the 2 cups of vegetable oil or ghee until smoking. Remove from the heat. Immerse the biscuits in the oil and let them fry, off the heat, for 5 minutes. Return the pan to a low heat and turn the biscuits over. Fry until golden brown. Remove the pan from the heat again and let them fry a few more minutes off the heat. Turn them again and return the pan to the heat. When the biscuits are brown, remove from the oil with a slotted spoon, letting the excess oil drip back into the pan. Drain further on paper towels.

Yield: 12 biscuits

# Rich Salted Biscuits
## (Khastaa Mathee)

1 cup unbleached white flour
1½ level teaspoons baking
   powder
½ teaspoon salt

6 teaspoons butter, chilled
7-9 teaspoons milk
1 teaspoon honey

---

¼ cup flour for dusting pastry
   board
¼ cup milk for brushing

½ teaspoon onion seeds or
   oregano (ajwan) seeds

1) In a bowl, sift together the flour, baking powder and salt. Add the butter, working it in with your fingertips. Mix in the milk and honey, forming a firm dough.

2) On a lightly floured (¼ cup, as needed) pastry board or flat surface, roll the dough out into ½ inch thick slab. Cut into rounds with a cookie cutter. Prick the top of each round with a fork.

3) Brush the top of each round with a little milk (from the ¼ cup) and sprinkle with onion seeds. Place on an ungreased cookie sheet and bake in a 300 degree oven 15 minutes or until golden brown.

Yield: 16 small biscuits

*More Tasty Snacks:*

# Banana with Chat Masala

An exotic evening snack. Good served with Yogi Tea, other salty snacks, or a sweet snack to balance the taste.

1 banana
1 lemon (juice only)

2 pinches of chat masala *

1) Peel the banana and cut in half lengthwise.

2) Squeeze the juice of one lemon onto each banana half and sprinkle with chat masala. *

*Chat masala can be purchased in Indian food stores or made fresh. To make chat masala: Mix together ¾ teaspoon ground roasted cumin seeds, ¼ teaspoon ground black pepper, ¼ teaspoon red chile powder, ¼ teaspoon ground asafoetida, ¼ teaspoon mango powder, ½ teaspoon black salt and ¾ teaspoon kosher or coarse salt.

Yield: 1 snack for 2 or 2 snacks for 1!

# Tofu Jalapeno Pancakes

Tofu, though not traditionally Indian, adapts itself very well to Indian cooking. These very spicy, hot pancakes are good for cold weather, prevention of flu, and for high energy. Very tasty!

| | |
|---|---|
| 2 cups garbanzo flour | 1¾ cups water |

| | |
|---|---|
| 1 large onion, chopped | ½ pound tofu, crumbled |
| 2 large green chiles, mild or hot, to taste | 1 teaspoon salt |
| 1 head garlic, chopped fine | 1 tablespoon oregano (ajwan) seeds |
| ¼ cup ginger, peeled and chopped fine | 2 tablespoons dry mint leaves, chopped |

¼-½ cup vegetable oil for
  frying

1) Mix garbanzo flour and water. Then combine with all other ingredients except oil.

2) In a frying pan, place enough oil for frying pancakes and heat to smoking point. Then lower the heat and begin frying pancakes, adding oil as necessary every few pancakes.

3) Serve piping hot with yogurt.

Yield: 13 3½-inch-wide pancakes.

# Spicy Cashews and Peanuts
## (Masaalaa Kaajoo ee Moongphoolee)

A "ready mix" to store or take anywhere.

2 teaspoons mango powder
3/4 teaspoon ground black
  pepper
1/2 teaspoon red chile powder

1/4 teaspoon black salt
1/2 teaspoon salt
2 teaspoons cumin powder
1/2 clove, crushed

---

1/4 cup ghee for frying
1/2 pound (1 1/2 cups) cashew
  nuts

1/2 pound (1 1/3 cups) raw
  peanuts, shelled

1) In a bowl, mix together the mango powder, black pepper, red chile, black salt, regular salt, cumin and crushed clove.

2) In a thick-bottomed frying pan, heat part of the ghee and fry the cashews on a low heat until golden. Remove the cashews, add more ghee if necessary, and fry the peanuts until golden. (When frying nuts, stir constantly and keep a sharp eye; they start to burn very suddenly.)

3) Remove the nuts from the ghee, place in a dry bowl, and immediately sprinkle with the spice mixture, tossing until all the nuts are well coated.

4) Place nut mixture in a large brown paper bag and shake well. Remove the nuts from the bag with a medium-sized strainer and place on a cookie sheet. (Excess spice mixture can be discarded or stored for future use.)

5) Cook the nuts in the oven for 5-8 minutes at 275 degrees (until crisp).

Yield: about 3 cups

# Yogurt Dishes, Soups and Salads

Yogurt dishes (raita) are an essential part of an Indian meal. Their coolness, smooth texture, white color and relatively mild taste serve as a refreshing oasis amid the many colorful, flavor-rich dishes.

When choosing which raita to serve with a meal, be sure to pick one that complements the main dish; a cool, fruit or mint raita goes well with a spicy vegetable, or a raita with vegetables and onions picks up a quieter rice or bean dish. Thick, rich, creamy yogurt makes the best raita.

Traditionally, soup and salad are not found in Indian cuisine, but with the free flow of East-West culture, modern India has created many wonderful soups and salads that have a distinctive Indian flair.

Cream of Almond Soup is very light in taste. For other light soups, you'll find that most dahl (bean) dishes, thinned out with a little extra water and liquefied in a food processor, can also serve as a soup course.

The salads can either start the meal, be served right along with the other main dishes the way raita is, or served as light meals in themselves.

# Cucumber Yogurt
## *(Kheeraa Raaitaa)*

2 cups yogurt
1 cup cucumber, peeled and
 grated
1 teaspoon cumin powder
1/2 teaspoon ground black
 pepper

1 tablespoon fresh coriander
 leaves, chopped
1/4 teaspoon nutmeg powder
1/2 teaspoon salt, or to taste

*too much pepper*

In a bowl, beat the yogurt with a whisk or an egg beater until it is creamy. Add the grated cucumber, cumin, black pepper, coriander leaves, nutmeg and salt and mix well. Chill before serving.

Yield: 2½ cups

# Baked Eggplant Yogurt
## *(Baigan Raaitaa)*

Eggplant dish:
1 small eggplant
vegetable oil to coat outside of
 eggplant
2 cups yogurt

1 teaspoon ground black
 pepper
1/2 teaspoon salt, or to taste

Garnish:
1 teaspoon cumin powder

1/4 teaspoon nutmeg powder

1) Preheat the oven to 350 degrees. Wash the eggplant, dry it off, oil the skin, and pierce it a few times with a knife. Place on a rack in the middle of the oven and bake until very soft (30-40 minutes).

2) Remove from the oven and let cool. Peel off the skin, place the pulp in a bowl and mash until smooth. Add the yogurt and mix well. Then stir in the black pepper and salt. Garnish with a sprinkling of cumin powder and nutmeg.

Yield: 2½ cups

# Festival Yogurt

## (Aaloo, Piaaz, Tamaatar, Poodeenaa Raaitaa)

Yogurt dish:
2 cups yogurt
1 medium onion, chopped
  fine
1 large tomato, chopped fine
1 medium potato, boiled,
  peeled and diced

1 small bunch mint leaves,
  chopped fine
1 teaspoon ground black
  pepper
1 teaspoon cumin seeds,
  roasted and ground
1/2 teaspoon salt, or to taste

Garnish:
1 pinch cumin powder

In a bowl, beat the yogurt with a whisk or an eggbeater until it is creamy. Add the onion, tomato, potato, mint, black pepper, cumin and salt and mix well. Garnish with a sprinkle of cumin powder.

Yield: 3½ cups

# Banana Yogurt
## (Kele Raaitaa)

Peppery sweet and sour in taste. Good with a bland rice dish.

2 cups yogurt
1/2 teaspoon ground black
  pepper
1 tablespoon honey
1/2 teaspoon lemon juice
1/4 teaspoon salt, or to taste

2 tablespoons raisins (which
  have been soaked in water
  for 10 minutes, then
  drained)
2 large bananas, peeled and
  sliced thin

In a bowl, beat the yogurt with a whisk or an eggbeater until it is creamy. Mix in the black pepper, honey, lemon juice, salt and raisins. Add the bananas and stir well, being careful not to mash them. Chill before serving.

Yield: about 2½ cups

# Spiced Potato Yogurt
## (Aaloo Raaitaa)

For a light meal, serve with vegetables.

Yogurt dish:
1 cup yogurt
1/2 teaspoon ground black
  pepper
1/4 teaspoon red chile powder
1/2 teaspoon cumin seeds,
  roasted and ground

1/4 teaspoon salt, or to taste
1/2 cup potatoes, boiled,
  peeled and sliced thin
additional cold milk, if
  necessary

Garnish:
1 teaspoon fresh coriander
  leaves, chopped

In a bowl, beat the yogurt with a whisk or an eggbeater until it is creamy. Add the black pepper, red chile powder, cumin and salt and mix well. Then add the potatoes and mix so that they are all covered with yogurt. (Note: If there is not enough yogurt, make up the difference with cold milk and stir it in well.) Garnish with coriander leaves. Chill for several hours before serving.

Yield: 1½ cups

# Mint Yogurt
## (Poodeenaa Raaitaa)

1/2 cup fresh mint leaves,
  chopped fine
1/2 cup fresh coriander leaves

3 tablespoons grated fresh
  coconut

6 green chiles, mild or hot, to
  taste, chopped

2 cups yogurt
1/2 teaspoon salt, or to taste

1/4 teaspoon nutmeg powder
  (optional)

1) In an electric blender, blend together the mint leaves, coriander leaves, coconut, green chiles and just enough water to let them blend well (¼ cup or less).

2) In a bowl, beat the yogurt with a whisk or an eggbeater until it is creamy. Add the blended ingredients, along with the salt and nutmeg and mix well. Serve chilled.

Yield: 2½-3 cups

# Mint Chutney Yogurt
## *(Poodeenaa Chatnee Raaitaa)*

*1 cup fresh mint leaves*
*2 tablespoons finely chopped*
  *peeled fresh ginger*
*1 small onion, quartered*
*2 - 4 green chiles, mild or hot,*
  *to taste*

*2 tablespoons lemon juice or*
  *1 tablespoon tamarind*
  *concentrate (seedless)*
*1 teaspoon cumin seeds*

---

*2 cups yogurt*
*ground black pepper (garnish)*

*2 teaspoons honey (optional)*

1) In an electric blender, blend together the mint leaves, ginger, onion, green chiles, cumin seeds and lemon juice or tamarind concentrate (with just enough water to let the ingredients blend well).

2) In a bowl, beat the yogurt with a whisk or an eggbeater until it is creamy. Add the blended ingredients and mix well. Garnish with a little black pepper sprinkled on top.

Note: If you want to make this raita sweet and sour, stir in the 2 teaspoons of honey.

Yield: 3 cups

# Peanut and Raisin Yogurt
## (Moongphalee Raaitaa)

Exotic texture and taste.

½ cup roasted peanuts,
   shelled
2 cups yogurt
¼ cup raisins (which have
   been soaked in water for 10
   minutes, then drained)

½ teaspoon ground black
   pepper
½ teaspoon red chile powder
¼ teaspoon salt, or to taste
1 tablespoon honey

Garnish:
½ teaspoon cumin powder

1) In an electric blender or coffee grinder, grind the peanuts to the consistency of meal.

2) In a bowl, beat the yogurt with a whisk or an eggbeater until it is creamy. Add the ground peanuts, raisins, black pepper, red chile, salt and honey. Stir well and garnish with a sprinkle of cumin powder. Serve with vegetables.

Yield: approximately 3 cups

# Crunchy Spicy Yogurt

2 cups yogurt
1 teaspoon ground black
   pepper
2-4 green chiles, mild or hot,
   to taste, chopped fine

1 teaspoon cumin seeds,
   roasted and ground
½ teaspoon salt, or to taste
½ cup milk
1 cup puffed rice

Garnish:
1 tablespoon fresh coriander
   leaves, chopped fine

In a bowl, beat the yogurt with a whisk or an eggbeater until it is creamy. Add the black pepper, green chiles, cumin, salt and milk and mix well. Then stir in the puffed rice. Garnish with coriander leaves. Chill for half an hour before serving.

Yield: 3 cups (serves 4-6)

## Soups and Salads:

# Yogurt Salad
## (Pachaadee)

A salad with a uniquely Indian taste.

| | |
|---|---|
| 4-5 small potatoes, peeled and diced | 1 cup green peas, fresh or frozen |

| | |
|---|---|
| 2 tomatoes | ½ cup peanuts, ground to a meal |
| 4 green chiles, mild or hot, to taste, chopped | 1 sprig fresh coriander leaves, chopped |
| 1 cup mung bean sprouts | 5 cups yogurt |
| ⅓ cup grated carrots | 1½ teaspoons salt, or to taste |
| ½ fresh coconut, grated | |

2 tablespoons vegetable oil
pinch of black mustard seed

1) Steam the potatoes and peas. Then, in a bowl, mix with the tomatoes, green chiles, sprouts, carrots, coconut, peanuts, coriander leaves, yogurt and salt.

2) In a thick-bottomed frying pan, heat the oil and saute the black mustard seeds until they start to pop. Add immediately to the yogurt mixture and stir. Serve chilled.

Yield: 9 cups

# Curried Cottage Cheese Salad

1/2 cup onions, sliced in
   crescents

1/2 teaspoon salt

---

2 tablespoons dried
   (unsweetened) coconut

4 tablespoons hot milk

---

1/2 green chile, mild or hot to
   taste, chopped coarsely
6 sprigs fresh coriander leaves
   or watercress (chopped
   coarsely)
1 cup cottage cheese

the juice of one lemon
1/4 teaspoon ground black
   pepper
1/2 bell pepper, chopped
   (optional)

1) Place the onions in a bowl and sprinkle with salt. Let stand 30 minutes, then pour cold water over them and drain well.

2) Soak the coconut in hot milk for 30 minutes. Then drain.

3) Mix the onions, coconut, green chile, coriander or watercress, cottage cheese, lemon juice, black pepper and (optional) bell pepper and stir well. Let stand 30 minutes before serving.

Yield: 2 cups

# Apple-Vegetable Salad

A most unusual hot salad — colorful and zesty!

1 cup green peas, fresh or
   frozen
1 carrot

1 small apple
1 medium potato

---

1/2 teaspoon mustard powder
1/2 teaspoon white pepper
1/4 teaspoon salt, or to taste

1/2 teaspoon lemon juice
3 teaspoons cream

1) Steam the green peas, carrot, apple and potato separately until each one is tender. Let them cool, then peel the potato, carrot and apple and dice. Place in a bowl.

2) Mix together the mustard powder, white pepper, salt, lemon juice and cream. Stir into the vegetables. Serve hot!

Yield: about 3½ cups

# Cream of Almond Soup

A very delicate soup, very good for children recuperating from an illness.

*1 cup milk*

---

*3 carrots*
*1 pound (about 3 cups)*
   *green peas, fresh or frozen*
*15 black peppercorns*

*1 inch piece fresh ginger,*
   *sliced*
*9 cups water*

---

*¼-½ teaspoon white*
   *pepper, to taste*

*4-5 teaspoons cornstarch*

---

*24 almonds*

---

*1 teaspoon salt, or to taste*

1) Boil milk, then let cool.

2) Wash, peel and cut the carrots into small pieces. In a large pot cook the peas, carrots, black peppercorns and fresh ginger in 9 cups of water, on a low heat, until only six cups of water are left. Then remove the vegetables, peppercorns and fresh ginger from the water.

3) To this broth add the white pepper and bring it to a boil. Mix the cornstarch in ⅓ cup of cold water and add it to the boiling water. Turn down the heat and stir until the mixture starts to thicken slightly. Then, in a blender, grind the almonds into the boiled, cooled milk.

4) Just before serving, add salt to taste.

Yield: 8 cups

# King Janak Plans a Feast

*Inspirational stories like this one are among those that were told to me as a child and which helped to shape my attitudes toward the art of preparing food.*

Janak, who ruled much of India in ancient times, was known as both the greatest king and the greatest yogi. It is said that to celebrate his fiftieth birthday he arranged a spectacular feast, the likes of which had never been seen before. Months in advance, he dispatched his royal cooks to all parts of the known world to collect the most delectable recipes that each region had to offer. Then he sent invitations to all the kings, princes and noblemen, to the greatest holy men and seers, and to representatives of the common people.

When the guests arrived at the great hall, they were astounded by the great variety and quantity of food that King Janak had set before them. Along the perimeters of the hall were long banquet tables, each of them filled with a colorful array of dishes from a different region. There was Italian food, Greek food, Arabian food; Persian, Tibetan and Chinese food; African food and Thai food; and of course a variety of delicacies from all over India. But the greatest astonishment was King Janak himself.

Seated on a dais with an eminent collection of heads of state, leaders of religious sects and honest, hardworking commoners, King Janak enjoyed his own meal — a half-filled bowl of rice with homemade yogurt. When asked why he abstained from the meal of a lifetime which he himself had arranged, King Janak stood up and replied, "I gathered together all the most delicious foods from all over the world and brought them to this meal — just to honor all of you, my friends. Then I gathered together all of my training, all of my discipline, and all of my self-restraint and brought those things to this meal as well. In this way I have honored myself."

# Vegetable Dishes

Vegetables (sabji or subzi) are center stage in the theater of Indian cooking. With the vast majority of her people strictly vegetarian, India has, over thousands of years, developed a vegetarian cuisine unequalled anywhere else in the world. The purpose of Indian vegetarian cooking is not to simulate the taste and appearance of meat, but to raise the presentation of the essential vegetable to its highest potential. Vegetables are cooked so that they smell extraordinary, look exquisite and taste delicious, as well as being hearty, satisfying and nourishing.

There are four major ways of preparing vegetable main dishes in India. In planning a meal with several dishes, it is nice to have a dish from each of these categories:

1) *The "wet" way* means with a sauce ("kari"). This is what is commonly referred to as curry. Curry powder, as sold in the stores, is almost never used in its preparation. Wet vegetable dishes usually contain two or more vegetables cooked or stewed together in a highly flavored, though not necessarily spicy, sauce. Sometimes the vegetables are in the form of balls ("koftas"), which have been deep fried before being cooked in the sauce.

2) *The "dry" way* is commonly referred to on restaurant menus as "bhujia" or "bhajia". This means there is no sauce. The vegetables are cooked by sauteing or frying with spices in a little *ghee* or vegetable oil. In a "dry" dish the onions and ginger would be sliced or chopped rather than grated or powdered.

3) *Stuffed vegetables* are just that: sturdy vegetables such as peppers, melons, even potatoes, that are scooped out, stuffed with a spice mixture, and then fried or baked.

4) When *rice or bean dishes* include vegetables, the vegetables are either cooked right along with the rice or beans, or cooked separately and added later on. Bean dishes (dahls) provide much of the protein of the Indian vegetarian diet, while rice dishes (pilau, pullao or baryani) provide much of the bulk. The recipes for rice and bean dishes are in separate chapters.

*Assorted Vegetable Dishes:*

# Cauliflower in Sauce
## (Masaalaa Gobee)

For those who love the spiciness of cloves, a unique dish for either lunch or dinner. Serve with an eggplant dish, greens and rice.

*1 cauliflower*

---

| | |
|---|---|
| *4 tomatoes, chopped* | *½ teaspoon salt, or to taste* |
| *2 teaspoons honey* | *½ teaspoon red chile powder* |

---

| | |
|---|---|
| *1 tablespoon ground black pepper* | *½ teaspoon black cardamon powder* |
| *½ teaspoon clove powder* | *3 whole bay leaves* |
| *½ teaspoon cinnamon powder* | *2 tablespoons fresh coriander leaves, chopped* |

1) Separate the cauliflower into fairly large pieces and steam them until tender. Remove from the heat and set aside.

2) In a large, thick-bottomed saucepan, mix together the tomatoes, honey, salt, red chile powder and a little water to make a tomato sauce. Cook until mushy.

3) Mix together the black pepper, cloves, cinnamon, black cardamon, bay leaves and coriander and add to the tomato sauce. Then add the cauliflower to the sauce and continue to cook until the sauce becomes thick.

Yield: 5 cups (6 servings)

# Whole Head Cauliflower Curry
## (Saabat Phoolgobhee)

*1 head cauliflower*

*2 medium onions*

*4 cloves garlic*

*1 inch fresh ginger, peeled and chopped*

*6 fresh green chiles, mild or hot to taste*

*4 whole cloves*

*2 green cardamon pods*

*1 small stick cinnamon*

*1/2 teaspoon salt, or to taste*

*1/2 teaspoon turmeric*

*1 stick butter (1/4 pound)*

*2 tablespoons water*

*1 cup yogurt*

*1 tablespoon fresh coriander leaves, chopped*

1) Thoroughly wash the whole cauliflower, carefully spreading the flowerets apart without breaking them. Steam the whole head for 5 minutes.

2) In an electric blender, blend the onions, garlic, ginger, green chiles, cloves, cardamon, cinnamon stick, salt and turmeric into a paste.

3) In a large, thick-bottomed frying pan, heat the butter. Add the paste and fry, stirring continuously. When it starts to stick, add the 2 tablespoons of water, continuing to cook and stir on a low heat. Add the yogurt and simmer for 5 minutes. Then remove from the heat.

4) Heat the oven to 350 degrees. In a baking pan, place the steamed cauliflower and pour the yogurt/spice mixture over it. Bake for 10 minutes until the cauliflower is tender. Remove from the oven and garnish with chopped coriander leaves.

Yield: about 4 cups

# Onion and Tomato Curry
## (Piaaz Tamaatar Sabjee)

A pungent and colorful side dish.

1 tablespoon vegetable oil or
   ghee
1/2 pound onions, sliced thin

5 cloves garlic, chopped
1 inch piece fresh ginger,
   peeled and chopped fine

---

5 green chiles, mild or hot, to
   taste, chopped
1/2 teaspoon turmeric
1/2 teaspoon garam masala

1 teaspoon cumin seeds
1/4 teaspoon salt, or to taste
1 small tomato, sliced thin

1) In a large, thick-bottomed frying pan or wok, heat the oil or ghee and saute the onions, garlic and ginger until light brown. (Add a little water, if necessary, to prevent dehydration while cooking.)

2) Add the green chiles, turmeric, garam masala, cumin and salt and stir well. Then add the tomato and cook on a low heat until the oil starts to separate out. (If it starts to stick, add a little water.)

Yield: 1 1/2 cups

# Eggplant Bhartha
## (Baigan Bharthaa)

1 very large eggplant or two
   small eggplants

---

2 teaspoons vegetable oil or
   ghee
1 large onion, chopped
1 inch piece fresh ginger,
   peeled and chopped fine

2 large tomatoes, chopped
1 teaspoon cumin powder
1/4 teaspoon salt, or to taste
1/8 teaspoon ground black
   pepper, or to taste

1) In the oven, broil the eggplant until the peel is charred and the inside is soft. Let it cool, peel and mash the pulp. Set aside.

2) In a large, thick-bottomed frying pan, heat the vegetable oil or ghee and saute the onions and ginger until the onions are golden, stirring frequently so the ginger doesn't stick. Add the tomatoes, cumin, salt and black pepper and continue to fry until the tomatoes are mushy. (Add water, if necessary, to prevent dehydration.)

3) Add the eggplant and keep cooking, stirring often, until the oil begins to separate out from the vegetables (about 10-15 minutes). Serve very hot.

Yield: 2 cups

# Stewed Tomatoes
## (Tamaatar Bharthaa)

A spicy side dish.

4 ripe tomatoes
1 large onion, chopped
2-3 green chiles, mild or hot,
   to taste, chopped

1 teaspoon salt, or to taste
1 tablespoon honey, or to
   taste

1) Peel the tomatoes by immersing them briefly in boiling water; the skins will shrivel up. Remove from the water, peel and, in a bowl, mash with a fork, removing any hard parts.

2) Add the onion and green chiles to the tomatoes. Add salt and honey and mix thoroughly.

Yield: 4 cups (serves 6)

# Chickpea Dahl Curry
## (Chanaa Daal Karee)

This spicy, satisfying dish is an unusual blend of flavors. Serve with plain rice.

| | |
|---|---|
| ½ cup lotus root | 7 cups water |
| ½ cup chickpeas (garbanzo beans) | |

| | |
|---|---|
| ½ cup eggplant, peeled and cubed | 1 tomato, chopped |
| ½ cup cauliflower, cut into small pieces | 12 green chiles, mild or hot, to taste, chopped fine |
| ½ cup green peas, fresh or frozen | 1 teaspoon salt, or to taste |
| 2 medium potatoes, peeled and cubed | 2 teaspoons turmeric |
| | 1 teaspoon crushed dry red chiles |

| | |
|---|---|
| ½ cup ghee or vegetable oil | 2 teaspoons mustard seeds |
| 2 teaspoons fenugreek seeds | 2 teaspoon cumin seeds |

| | |
|---|---|
| ½ cup tamarind concentrate, seedless | 4 teaspoons fresh coriander leaves, chopped |

1) If the lotus root is dry, it should be *soaked overnight*. (Canned lotus root need not be soaked.) Also, clean and soak the chickpeas in 7 cups of water *overnight*. In the morning, wash, peel and cut the lotus root into small pieces. Cook the chickpeas in the water in which they were soaked, along with the lotus root pieces. When the chickpeas have become very soft, remove the lotus root pieces from the water and set them aside in a bowl. Strain off the water from the chickpeas and set aside.

2) In a large, thick-bottomed pot, place the chickpeas, 8 cups of water (including chickpea water), salt, turmeric, red chiles and all the chopped vegetables except the lotus root. Cook on a low heat until all the vegetables are soft. Then add the cooked lotus root. Set aside.

3) In a thick-bottomed frying pan, heat the vegetable oil or ghee and saute the fenugreek seeds, mustard seeds and cumin seeds. Add the tamarind and coriander leaves and cook for 5 minutes. Pour this mixture over the chickpea-vegetable mixture and serve.

Yield: 8 cups

# Leek Bhajia

A mild complement, sweet and light, for any meal.

| | |
|---|---|
| 2 medium leeks | 1 teaspoon turmeric |
| 2 teaspoons butter | 1/2 teaspoon ginger powder |
| 1/2 teaspoon cumin seeds | 1/4 teaspoon salt, or to taste |

1/2 teaspoon garam masala

1) Carefully wash the leeks and slice into thin rounds. Soak in water for 10 minutes, then rinse thoroughly and drain off all the water.

2) In a thick-bottomed frying pan or wok, melt the butter and add the cumin seeds, sauteing for a few seconds (making sure they don't burn). Then add the turmeric, ginger, salt and leeks. Continue to fry for 3-4 minutes, then add a little water, cover and cook over a low heat until the leeks are tender.

3) Drain off any left-over water and sprinkle the leeks with garam masala before serving.

Yield: 2 cups

# Chickpea Flour Curry
## (Sindhee Karee)

A mild curry with interesting textures. Serve with plain rice and a spicy chutney.

*2 large lotus roots*

| | |
|---|---|
| *2 tablespoons tamarind concentrate (seedless)* | *4 tablespoons warm water* |

| | |
|---|---|
| *2 potatoes*<br>*1 small eggplant* | *1/2 head cauliflower* |

| | |
|---|---|
| *2-3 tablespoons vegetable oil or ghee* | *3/4 cup chickpea (garbanzo) flour* |

| | |
|---|---|
| *4 cups water*<br>*2 tablespoons turmeric* | *3/4 teaspoon salt, or to taste* |

| | |
|---|---|
| *1 tablespoon vegetable oil or ghee*<br>*1 tablespoon fenugreek seeds*<br>*2 teaspoons white cumin seeds*<br>*1/2 cup green peas, fresh or frozen*<br>*3 green chiles, mild or hot, to taste, chopped* | *4 whole dried red chiles*<br>*2 tablespoons fresh coriander leaves, chopped*<br>*a few fresh mint leaves, chopped*<br>*1 large tomato, chopped* |

| | |
|---|---|
| *2 tablespoons vegetable oil or ghee* | *1 tablespoon mustard seeds* |

1) If the lotus root is dry, soak it in water *overnight*.

2) Dissolve the tamarind concentrate in 4 tablespoons of warm water.

3) Wash the potatoes and cut into large pieces. Peel the eggplant and cut into medium pieces. Wash the cauliflower and divide into medium-size flowerets. Scrape and wash the lotus root and cut into big pieces. Wash again thoroughly. Set the vegetables aside.

4) In a large, thick-bottomed saucepan, heat 2-3 tablespoons of vegetable oil or ghee and fry the chickpea flour until light brown, being careful not to let it burn. Then slowly add 4 cups water, *stirring continuously* to avoid lumping, and add the turmeric, salt and lotus root. Continue cooking on medium heat until half the liquid is gone.

5) In a thick-bottomed frying pan, heat some oil or ghee and fry the fenugreek seeds and white cumin seeds until brown. Add them to the sauce, along with the potatoes, eggplant, cauliflower, peas, green chiles, red chiles and fresh coriander leaves. Then add the mint leaves, chopped tomatoes and tamarind water. Simmer for a few more minutes.

6) In a thick-bottomed frying pan, heat some oil or ghee and fry the mustard seeds until they start popping. Add to the curry, mixing thoroughly.

Yield: 6 cups

# Creamy Spinach and Cheese
## (Saag Paneer)

panir from 2 quarts of milk
(see recipe, p. 24) or 1½
pounds tofu

2 tablespoons ghee

---

1 tablespoon ghee
1 cup chopped onion
1 tablespoon ginger powder

5 cloves garlic
2 whole cloves
1 cup water

---

¼ teaspoon baking soda
1 teaspoon salt, or to taste
½ cup water

2½ pounds (4 large bunches)
spinach, washed and
chopped

---

1 teaspoon red chile powder
2 teaspoons cumin powder
2 teaspoons coriander powder
⅛ teaspoon nutmeg

3 medium tomatoes, peeled
and chopped
½ cup cottage cheese
½ cup water

1) Cut the panir into small cubes. (Tofu can be used as a simple, though less authentic, substitute.) In a large, thick-bottomed saucepan, heat the ghee and fry the panir gently until light brown. Remove the panir with a slotted spoon, letting the excess ghee drip back into the pan. Set aside.

2) Add 1 tablespoon ghee and fry the onions until transparent. Then add the ginger, garlic, cloves and 1 cup of water. Mix thoroughly and cook until the water evaporates.

3) Add the baking soda, salt to taste, 1/2 cup of water and chopped spinach. Mix thoroughly and cook for 5 minutes.

4) Add the chile powder, cumin, coriander, nutmeg, tomatoes, cottage cheese, fried panir and another ½ cup water. Cook on a low heat until the panir is soft and the ghee begins to separate out.

Yield: 6 cups

# Ripe Mango Curry
## (Amb Dee Sabjee)

Delicious, spicy, with an unusual blend of tastes.

*4 large ripe mangoes*

---

| | |
|---|---|
| *2 tablespoons vegetable oil or ghee* | *4 whole dry red chiles* |
| *1 teaspoon mustard seeds* | *1 cup coconut, grated* |
| | *1 teaspoon turmeric* |

---

| | |
|---|---|
| *1½ cups water* | *1 tablespoon honey* |
| *¼ cup raisins* | *2 bay leaves* |
| *4 whole cloves* | *½ teaspoon salt, or to taste* |

1) Peel the mangoes and cut into small pieces.

2) In a large, thick-bottomed frying pan or wok, heat the oil or ghee and fry the mustard seeds and red chiles until they start to snap and crackle, being careful not to let them burn. Then mix in the grated coconut and turmeric and fry until light brown, stirring continuously.

3) Add the mangoes, water, raisins, cloves, honey, bay leaves and salt. Simmer on a low heat for 10 minutes, stirring now and then. Note: This dish may be reheated and served the following day when it will taste spicier.

Yield: 8 cups (serves 8)

# Pineapple Curry
## (Anaanaas Sabjee)

An exotic side dish, easy to prepare and good with plain rice.

1 teaspoon coriander seeds
4 whole, dry red chiles
2 tablespoons vegetable oil or
  ghee

½ teaspoon mustard seeds
1 large onion, chopped

---

1 large pineapple, peeled and
  cut into small pieces
2 tablespoons honey

½ teaspoon salt, or to taste
1 pint water

1) Grind the coriander seeds and red chiles to a paste.

2) In a large, thick-bottomed frying pan or wok, heat the vegetable oil or ghee and fry the mustard seeds and onion until light brown. Add the coriander/chile paste and stir well.

3) Add the pineapple pieces and stir well. Add the honey, salt and water. Cook on a low heat until the sauce is thickened.

Yield: 4 cups

# Yam Curry
## *(Arbee Bhujiaa)*

Yams with a distinctly Indian flavor.

*2 medium-sized yams*

---

| | |
|---|---|
| *2 tablespoons oregano seeds* | *½ tablespoon ghee* |

---

| | |
|---|---|
| *⅓ tablespoon ghee* | *1 teaspoon garam masala* |
| *½ teaspoon turmeric* | *2-3 green chiles, mild or hot,* |
| *1 tablespoon white cumin* | *to taste, chopped fine* |
| *seeds* | *½ teaspoon salt, or to taste* |
| *1 teaspoon fresh ginger,* | *¼ teaspoon ground black* |
| *peeled and finely chopped* | *pepper* |

---

*5 teaspoons mango powder*

---

Garnish:

| | |
|---|---|
| *1 small tomato, chopped* | *2 teaspoons fresh coriander leaves, chopped* |

1) Boil or bake the yams until tender but not mushy. Then peel and flatten the whole yam by pressing with your hands (or slice).

2) Sprinkle the yam with oregano seeds. In a large frying pan, heat ½ tablespoon of ghee and fry the yams until they are golden brown.

3) Add another ⅓ tablespoon of ghee and mix in the turmeric, white cumin, garam masala, ginger, green chiles, salt and black pepper. Cook for a few minutes.

4) When ready to serve, add the mango powder and cook for another minute or two.

5) Place on a serving dish and garnish with chopped tomato and coriander leaves.

Yield: 2 cups

# Royal Potato Curry
## (Shaahee Aaloo Sabjee)

Fresh coconut and coriander make this dish a delight.

For the potato balls:

6 medium potatoes

1 teaspoon salt
water for boiling the potatoes

---

1 tablespoon ghee, melted
2 green chiles, mild or hot, to
   taste, chopped very fine

1 teaspoon ginger powder

---

1/2 teaspoon salt, or to taste
4 tablespoons unbleached
   white flour

2 cups vegetable oil or ghee
   for deep frying

---

For the curry:

2 teaspoons white poppy
   seeds

water to cover poppy seeds

---

4 green cardamon pods (use
   only the seeds)
2 tablespoons almonds

2 tablespoons grated coconut
   (fresh, if possible)
3-4 cups milk

---

1 tablespoon cornstarch

---

3 green chiles, mild or hot, to
   taste, chopped
1/2 teaspoon red chile powder
1/2 teaspoon white pepper
   powder

2 small tomatoes, chopped
1/2 teaspoon salt, or to taste

---

2 teaspoons fresh coriander
   leaves, chopped

*To make the potato balls:*
1) Boil the potatoes in water with 1 teaspoon salt until tender. Remove from the water, peel and mash. Set aside to cool.

2) Add the tablespoon of melted ghee, green chiles, ginger powder and ½ teaspoon salt and mix thoroughly. Form this mixture into small balls, about the size of a walnut.

3) In a bowl, add enough water to the flour to make a thin batter. Dip the potato balls in the batter.

4) In a thick-bottomed saucepan, heat the 2 cups of vegetable oil or ghee to smoking point. Carefully immerse the potato balls in the hot oil and deep fry until brown. Remove with a slotted spoon, letting the excess oil drip back into the pan. Drain the balls further on paper towels.

*To make the curry:*
1) Soak the white poppy seeds for 10 minutes in just enough water to cover them.

2) In an electric blender, blend the white poppy seeds. Then blend in the green cardamon seeds, almonds, coconut and milk.

3) In a thick-bottomed saucepan or wok, bring this mixture to a boil. Mix the cornstarch with enough milk (from step 2) to form a paste, and then add this paste to the rest of the boiling milk, mixing thoroughly. Continue cooking and stirring until the sauce thickens.

4) When thick, add the green chile powder, red chile powder, white pepper and tomatoes and stir well. Add the fried potato balls, mixing them in carefully so they don't break. Add ½ teaspoon of salt.

5) Garnish with chopped coriander leaves.

Yield: approximately 48 balls and 5 cups of curry

# Kashmiri Steamed Potatoes
## (Kashmeeree Dum Aaloo)

Delicate and distinctive in flavor. A gourmet delight!

1 teaspoon red chile powder
1 teaspoon ginger powder
1 teaspoon anise seed powder

1 teaspoon fresh coriander
  leaves, chopped
1 teaspoon turmeric
½ teaspoon salt

---

2 green chiles, mild or hot, to
  taste, chopped fine

¾ teaspoon garam masala
pinch of nutmeg

---

8 very small potatoes

---

½ cup mustard oil

pinch of asafoetida

---

¾ cup yogurt

½ cup water

1) Measure out chile powder, ginger powder, anise powder, chopped coriander, turmeric and salt and set aside in a small bowl.

2) Mix together chopped chiles, garam masala and nutmeg. Reserve in a small bowl.

3) Boil the potatoes. When tender, remove from the water, peel and set aside.

4) Reserve 2 tablespoons mustard oil. In a thick-bottomed frying pan or wok, heat the remaining oil until smoking. Fry the whole boiled potatoes until golden brown. Remove from the oil and prick them all over with a toothpick. Discard oil from pan and wipe the pan clean with a paper towel.

5) In a frying pan, heat 2 tablespoons of oil reserved earlier. Remove from the heat and add the asafoetida and stir until it swells. Then crush it to a powder and reheat, adding the bowl of chile powder, ginger, anise, coriander, turmeric and salt. In a bowl, beat the yogurt slightly to thicken it, then add to the spice mixture along with ½ cup of water. Simmer for 15 minutes.

6) Add the potatoes and continue to simmer on low heat until the sauce thickens (about 10 minutes). Sprinkle with garam masala, nutmeg and green chile mixture before serving.

Yield: 2½ cups

# Dry Potato Curry
## (Subhaa Aaloo Sabjee)

Best served with yogurt.

*3 medium potatoes, peeled
  and cubed*

| | |
|---|---|
| *6 tablespoons vegetable oil or ghee* | *2 teaspoons cumin seeds* |
| *2 teaspoons mustard seeds* | *1 teaspoon crushed dry red chiles* |
| *2 teaspoons oregano seeds* | *½ teaspoon salt, or to taste* |

*a few fresh coriander leaves*

1) Steam the cubed potatoes until tender. Set aside.

2) In a large, thick-bottomed frying pan or wok, heat the vegetable oil or ghee, then add the mustard, oregano and cumin seeds, stir well and add the red chiles and salt.

3) Add the steamed potatoes, continuing to stir as they cook for a few minutes longer. Then garnish with coriander leaves before serving.

Yield: 2 cups (3 servings)

# Bengali Style Cabbage and Potatoes
## (Band Gobee Aaloo)

A good filler course for serving a large group.

| | |
|---|---|
| 2 medium potatoes | ¼-½ cup ghee |

| | |
|---|---|
| 1 small cabbage | ½ teaspoon ginger powder |
| 1 teaspoon turmeric | 1 teaspoon red chile powder |

| | |
|---|---|
| ½ cup tomatoes, peeled and quartered | ½ teaspoon honey |
| | 1 teaspoon salt, or to taste |

Topping:
½ teaspoon clove powder
½ teaspoon cinnamon
   powder

½ teaspoon cardamon
   powder

1) Peel and cut the potatoes into quarters. In a deep, thick-bottomed frying pan or wok, heat the ghee and fry the potatoes until light brown. Then remove from the ghee and set aside.

2) Shred the cabbage and fry in the remaining ghee, adding the turmeric, ginger and red chile powder. Stir frequently to avoid sticking.

3) Peel the tomatoes (easily done by dipping them in boiling water for a few minutes; the skin will shrivel off) and cut into quarters. Add the tomatoes, potatoes, honey and salt to the cooking cabbage. Cover and cook over a low heat until all the vegetables are tender. If necessary, add a little water to prevent scorching.

4) When everything is fully cooked, sprinkle with the clove, cinnamon and cardamon powders and serve.

Yield: 9 cups

# Potato and Tomato Curry
## (Aaloo Tamaatar Sabjee)

| | |
|---|---|
| 3 medium potatoes | water to cover potatoes |

| | |
|---|---|
| 4 tablespoons vegetable oil or ghee<br>2 large onions, sliced | 2 tablespoons fresh ginger, peeled and finely chopped |

| | |
|---|---|
| 1 teaspoon turmeric<br>1 teaspoon red chile powder | 1 teaspoon cumin seeds<br>2 medium tomatoes, chopped |

| | |
|---|---|
| 1 teaspoon salt | 2 cups water |

| | |
|---|---|
| 2 teaspoons garam masala | a few fresh coriander leaves |

1) Peel the potatoes and dice in small cubes. Keep them immersed in cold water to prevent discoloration.

2) In a large, thick-bottomed frying pan, heat the vegetable oil or ghee and saute the onions and ginger until golden brown. Then add the turmeric, red chile powder, cumin seeds and tomatoes. Mix thoroughly and fry for 2 minutes.

3) Add the potato cubes and fry for 1 minute, stirring continuously. Then add the salt and water and simmer on a low heat until the potatoes are soft and start to crumble. A thick sauce will form. Sprinkle with garam masala and garnish with coriander leaves.

Yield: 3 cups (serves 4-6)

# String Beans and Potatoes
## (Faleeaan Aaloo)

Very hardy and satisfying; well complemented by tomato curry.

1/3-1/2 cup vegetable oil or ghee
1 onion, chopped

1 inch fresh ginger, peeled and chopped fine

---

1/2 teaspoon turmeric
1/2 teaspoon crushed dry red chiles
3 green chiles, mild or hot, to taste, chopped
1/2 teaspoon salt, or to taste

1/2 pound green beans (string beans) (about 1 1/2 cups)
1/2 cup water
1 medium potato, peeled and diced

---

1/2 teaspoon coriander powder

1) In a large, thick-bottomed saucepan, heat the vegetable oil or ghee and saute the onions and ginger until light brown. Then add, one by one stirring after each, the turmeric, crushed dry red chiles, green chiles, and salt. Add the green beans, 1/2 cup water and potatoes and cook until potatoes are tender (approximately 10 minutes). If necessary, add a little more water and cook until it is a "dry" vegetable mixture.

2) Stir for 1 minute, sprinkle with coriander and let sit for 5 minutes.

Yield: 4 cups

*Green Pea Dishes:*

# Mushroom and Pea Curry
## (Khumbaa Matar)

A very tasty dish!

¼ cup vegetable oil or ghee
2 large onions, sliced
5 cloves garlic, chopped

1 inch piece fresh ginger,
    peeled and chopped fine

---

½ teaspoon turmeric
½ teaspoon red chile powder
1 tablespoon garam masala
¼ teaspoon nutmeg

1 teaspoon salt, or to taste
3 medium tomatoes, chopped
    or 2 tablespoons tomato
    paste

---

½ pound mushrooms (about
    18 medium-sized
    mushrooms), washed and
    cut into large slices

1 cup water
½ pound green peas, fresh or
    frozen (about 1½ cups)

1) In a large, thick-bottomed saucepan or wok, heat the oil or ghee and saute the onions, garlic and ginger until golden brown. Add the turmeric, red chile powder, garam masala, nutmeg and salt and stir well. Then add the tomatoes or tomato paste and continue cooking and stirring until the oil begins to separate out.

2) Add the mushrooms and mix well. Then add 1 cup of water, cover and cook on a medium heat until the mushrooms are half done. Add the peas, mix well and cover. Simmer on a low heat, being careful not to let the mixture burn.

3) After all the liquid is gone, continue cooking, stirring continuously, until the oil starts to separate out. Remove from the heat and serve.

Yield: 4 - 5 cups

# Pea and Potato Curry
## *(Aaloo Matar)*

A nice dish for formal occasions.

1 pound (about 3 cups) green
  peas, fresh or frozen
  (defrosted)
1 medium potato, boiled and
  peeled
1 teaspoon poppy seeds

1/2 teaspoon crushed dry red
  chiles
1 teaspoon garam masala
1/2 cup chickpea (garbanzo)
  flour
1 teaspoon salt, or to taste

---

2 cups vegetable oil or ghee
  for deep frying

---

2 tablespoons vegetable oil or
  ghee for sauteing
2 large onions, chopped fine

1 clove garlic, chopped
1 inch piece fresh ginger,
  peeled and chopped fine

---

1 tomato, chopped fine
1/2 teaspoon turmeric

1 teaspoon coriander powder
3 cups water

---

1/2 teaspoon coriander powder

1) Mash the peas and boiled potato together. Add the poppy seeds, red chiles, garam masala, chickpea flour and salt. Mix well to form a thick paste. With this paste form small balls about the size of a walnut.

2) In a thick-bottomed saucepan or wok, heat the 2 cups of vegetable oil or ghee to smoking point. Carefully immerse the balls in the hot oil and deep fry at a low temperature until brown. If the cooking temperature is too high, the chickpea flour will not cook thoroughly. Remove with a slotted spoon, letting the excess oil drip back into the pan. Drain further on paper towels.

3) In a thick-bottomed frying pan, heat the vegetable oil or ghee and saute the onions, garlic and ginger until golden brown. Add the tomatoes, turmeric and 1 teaspoon of coriander powder; mix well, then add the water and cook for 5 minutes.

4) Put the deep fried balls in a flat casserole and pour sauce over them. Do not stir. Cook 1 more minute. Then turn off the heat, sprinkle with ½ teaspoon of coriander powder, and keep covered at low heat in the oven until ready to serve.

Yield: about 7 cups

# Carrot and Pea Curry
## (Gaajar Matar)

Fast, colorful and delicious!

½ cup vegetable oil or ghee
1 large onion, chopped
1 tablespoon finely chopped
  peeled fresh ginger
½ teaspoon salt, or to taste
¼ teaspoon ground black
  pepper

1 teaspoon oregano seeds
½ teaspoon crushed dry red
  chiles
¼ teaspoon turmeric
1 tablespoon tomato paste
2 tablespoons water

---

2 medium carrots, peeled and
  cut in ¼ inch slices

½ pound (about 1½ cups)
  green peas, fresh or frozen

1) In a large, thick-bottomed frying pan or wok, heat the oil or ghee and saute the onions and ginger until brown. Add the salt, black pepper, oregano seeds, red chiles and turmeric and stir well. Add the tomato paste and 2 tablespoons of water. Stir and cook for 1 minute.

2) Add the carrots and peas and a cup of water. Cover and cook until the carrots and peas are soft. (If using frozen peas, don't add them until the carrots are half done.)

3) When the water is completely absorbed, continue cooking and stirring the curry until the oil starts to separate out.

Yield: 2½ cups

# Pea and Cheese Curry
## (Matar Paneer)

The very tasty sweet and spicy sauce of this dish sets it in a class by itself.

½ pound panir (see recipe p. 24) or tofu (soybean curd)

2 cups vegetable oil or ghee for deep frying

---

2 large onions
6 cloves garlic
½ teaspoon turmeric

¼ teaspoon mustard seeds
1 teaspoon cumin seeds
1 teaspoon poppy seeds

---

½ cup vegetable oil or ghee for frying
2 tablespoons tomato paste (or 2 tomatoes, chopped fine)

2 tablespoons water

---

3 inch piece fresh ginger, peeled and chopped fine
¼ teaspoon green cardamon seeds
½ teaspoon crushed dry red chiles

¼ teaspoon nutmeg powder
2 bay leaves
½ teaspoon salt, or to taste

---

1 pint water

½ pound green peas, fresh or frozen (about 1½ cups)

1) Cut the panir (or tofu) into small cubes. In a thick-bottomed saucepan or wok, heat the 2 cups of oil or ghee for deep frying. Deep fry the panir or tofu cubes until golden brown. Remove with a slotted spoon, letting the excess oil drip back into the pan. Set aside.

2) In an electric blender, grind together the onion, garlic, turmeric, mustard seeds, cumin seeds and poppy seeds, making a fine paste without using any water.

3) In a thick-bottomed frying pan, heat the vegetable oil or ghee and fry this paste, stirring continuously, until brown. Then add the tomato paste (or tomatoes) and 2 tablespoons of water. Keep stirring and cooking until the oil starts to separate out.

4) Add the ginger, green cardamon seeds, red chiles, nutmeg, bay leaves and salt. Stir thoroughly and add the deep fried panir (or tofu) cubes. Let simmer on a low heat for 2 minutes, stirring frequently to prevent sticking.

5) Add the water and peas and cook on a low heat for 10 minutes until the peas are tender.

Yield: 3 cups

# Cabbage and Pea Curry
## (Band Gobee Matar Sabjee)

Good with plain rice or dahl.

| | |
|---|---|
| 4 tablespoons vegetable oil or ghee | 5 cloves garlic, chopped fine |
| 1 large onion, chopped | 2 inch piece fresh ginger, peeled and chopped fine |

| | |
|---|---|
| 5 green chiles, mild or hot, to taste, chopped fine | 1/2 teaspoon salt, or to taste |
| 1 teaspoon crushed dry red chiles | |

| | |
|---|---|
| 1/2 small cabbage head, shredded fine | 1/2 cup water |
| 1 cup (about 5 ounces) green peas, fresh or frozen | |

1) In a large, thick-bottomed frying pan or wok, heat the vegetable oil or ghee and fry the onion, garlic and ginger until light brown. Add green chiles, red chiles and salt and stir for 1/2 minute.

2) Add the shredded cabbage, peas and 1/2 cup water. Cover and cook on a low heat until tender. Uncover and turn up the heat, frying the mixture until the oil starts to separate out. Stir and serve hot.

Yield: about 2 cups

# White Squash Curry
## (Gheeaa Sabjee)

Excellent with lotus root kofta curry.

*3 - 5 white squash ("patty pan")*

| | |
|---|---|
| 3 tablespoons vegetable oil or ghee | 1 inch fresh ginger, peeled and chopped fine |
| 2 medium onions, sliced | 1 teaspoon oregano seeds (ajwan) |
| 6 cloves garlic, chopped | |

| | |
|---|---|
| 1 medium tomato, chopped | 4 green chiles, mild or hot, to taste, chopped |
| ½ teaspoon turmeric | ½ teaspoon salt, or to taste |
| 2 bay leaves | |
| ½ teaspoon crushed dry red chiles | |

| | |
|---|---|
| 1 cup water | 1 teaspoon garam masala |

1) Peel the white squash and cut into small pieces.

2) In a large, thick-bottomed frying pan, heat the vegetable oil or ghee and saute the onions, garlic, ginger and oregano seeds until golden brown.

3) Add the tomato and stir well. Then add the turmeric, bay leaves, red chiles, green chiles and salt, stir thoroughly, and cook until the oil starts to separate out.

4) Add the chopped squash, stir and add 1 cup of water. Cover and simmer until the squash is tender and all the water is absorbed. Then cook for a short while longer and sprinkle with garam masala before serving.

Yield: 2 - 3½ cups

# Pumpkin Bhartha: Sweet and Sour
## (Khataa Pethaa)

The exotic sweet and spicy flavor of this dish is well complemented by a bland or salty dish.

*2 tablespoons tamarind concentrate (or 2 table-spoons mango powder)*

*½ cup warm water*
*1 pound pumpkin*

---

*2 tablespoons vegetable oil or ghee*
*2 large onions, chopped*

*1 tablespoon fresh ginger, chopped and peeled*

---

*¼ teaspoon turmeric*
*½ teaspoon mustard seeds*
*6 green chiles, mild or hot, to taste, chopped fine*

*1½ cups water*

---

*⅛ cup honey*

---

*1 tablespoon fresh coriander leaves, chopped*

1) Soak the tamarind or mango powder in ½ cup warm water and set aside.

2) Peel the pumpkin and cut into small pieces.

3) In a thick-bottomed saucepan or wok, heat the oil or ghee, add the onions and ginger and fry until brown. Add the turmeric, mustard seeds, green chiles and stir well. Add the pumpkin pieces, continuing to stir. Then add 1½ cups of water and cook until the pumpkin is tender (adding more water if necessary to avoid scorching).

4) Add the tamarind water (step 1) and the honey to the cooking pumpkin mixture. Keep cooking, stirring frequently, until all the water is evaporated and the oil starts to separate out. Garnish with chopped coriander leaves.

Yield: 2½ cups

# Bitter Melon with Yogurt
## (Karelaa Dahee)

A rare treat!

4-6 medium-sized bitter
  melons

salt for sprinkling on melon

---

¼ cup vegetable oil or ghee
  for frying
3 large onions, chopped
  coarsely

1 tablespoon finely chopped
  garlic
1 tablespoon finely chopped
  peeled fresh ginger

---

1 teaspoon cumin powder
1 teaspoon coriander powder
1 teaspoon turmeric
½ teaspoon crushed dry red
  chiles

½ teaspoon salt, or to taste
1 cup yogurt

1) Without peeling the bitter melons, cut them into thin slices. Sprinkle with salt and mix well. *Let sit in a bowl for half an hour,* then wash thoroughly and squeeze out the water with your hands. Let them sit for another 5 minutes to allow any excess water to drain off. Set aside.

2) In a thick-bottomed frying pan, heat the vegetable oil or ghee and fry the chopped onions, garlic and ginger until golden brown. Then add the cumin, coriander, turmeric and crushed dry red chiles, salt and yogurt, stirring continuously. When the oil starts to separate out from the mixture, remove from the heat.

3) In a separate frying pan, fry the bitter melon in vegetable oil or ghee until light brown. Then add it to the onion/yogurt mixture and simmer for a few more minutes.

Yield: 3 cups

# Bitter Melon and Onions
## (Karelaa Piaaz)

2-3 medium-sized bitter
melons

salt for sprinkling on bitter
melons

---

2 cups vegetable oil or ghee
for deep frying

---

6 small onions
1 teaspoon chile powder, mild
or spicy, to taste

1 tablespoon mango powder
1/2 teaspoon salt

1) Scrape and peel the bitter melon and cut into small pieces. Place in a bowl, sprinkle with salt and mix well. *Let sit for 1 hour.* Then wash the bitter melon thoroughly and squeeze out the water with your hands. Let sit in the bowl another 5 minutes so any excess water can drain off.

2) In a large, thick-bottomed saucepan, heat the oil or ghee and deep fry the bitter melon on a medium heat. Keep stirring to make sure the bitter melon fries evenly to a golden brown. Remove with a slotted spoon, letting the excess oil drip back into the pan. Set aside.

3) Chop the onions in quarters. Deep fry in the same oil until light brown. Remove from the oil with a slotted spoon, letting the excess oil drip back into the pan.

4) In a bowl, mix together the bitter melon and the onions, add the chile powder, mango powder and salt, stir well and serve.

Yield: 3 cups

## Vegetable Koftas in Sauce:

"Koftas" are deep-fried vegetable balls. Easy-to make, they are a deliciously different way of preparing vegetables.

# Lotus Root Kofta Curry
## (Kanwal Kakree Koftaa)

Lotus root makes this dish enchantingly sweet.

2 pounds lotus root
3/4 cup chickpea (garbanzo)
   flour
1 teaspoon salt, or to taste
1/2 teaspoon baking soda
1 teaspoon red chile powder
2 teaspoons garam masala

1 teaspoon oregano seeds
   (ajwan)
8 green chiles, mild or hot, to
   taste, chopped
2 cups vegetable oil or ghee
   for deep frying

---

1/4 cup vegetable oil or ghee
   for sauteing
4 large onions, chopped

8 cloves garlic, chopped
1/2 cup fresh ginger, peeled and
   chopped fine

---

2 large tomatoes, chopped
1 teaspoon cumin powder
2 teaspoons turmeric

2 teaspoons coriander powder
1/2 cup yogurt

---

2 cups water

1/2 teaspoon coriander powder

1) If the lotus root is dry, soak it *overnight*.

2) Scrape and wash the lotus root and cut into small pieces. Wash again thoroughly. In an electric blender, blend the lotus root with enough water to form a smooth paste. Add the chickpea (garbanzo) flour, salt, baking soda, red chile, garam masala, oregano seeds and green chiles. Mix until a thick paste is formed. Use this paste to form small balls about the size of a walnut, squeezing out excess water as you form them to help them adhere.

3) In a thick-bottomed saucepan or wok, heat the 2 cups of vegetable oil or ghee. Deep fry the lotus root balls on a medium heat until light brown. Remove with a slotted spoon, letting the excess oil drip back into the pan, and set aside.

4) In a thick-bottomed frying pan, heat the vegetable oil or ghee and saute the onions, garlic and ginger until brown. Then add the tomatoes, cumin, turmeric and 2 teaspoons of coriander powder. Fry for 2 minutes, add the yogurt and simmer for 5 more minutes.

5) Add 2 cups of water and boil for 5 minutes. Then add the lotus root koftas and simmer for 2 minutes on a low heat. Before serving, sprinkle with ½ teaspoon of coriander powder.

Yield: 48 balls in 3½ cups sauce

# Golden Flower Koftas
## (Nargaasee Koftaa Sabjee)

A fancy party main dish good with plain rice and dahl. *Nargaasee* is the Indian name for the narcissus flower. This dish is named for that flower because the colorful gold and white balls, cut in half and arranged on a platter, resemble that flower in bloom.

For the koftas:

1 pound lotus root (4 to six-inch long roots) or 2 medium potatoes

salted water to soak lotus root (if used)

---

2 green chiles, mild or hot, to taste, chopped

2 tablespoons chickpea (garbanzo) flour

1/2 teaspoon garam masala

1 teaspoon cumin powder

1 teaspoon fresh coriander leaves, chopped

6 almonds, soaked, peeled and crushed

panir from 2 quarts of milk, mashed (about 1 1/2 pounds panir) (see recipe p. 24)

---

4 teaspoons turmeric for coloring

2 cups vegetable oil or ghee for deep frying

---

For the curry:

3 teaspoons vegetable oil or ghee for sauteing

1 cup chopped onions

6 cloves garlic, chopped

2 teaspoons fresh ginger, peeled and finely chopped

1 cup water

1 teaspoon crushed, dry red chiles

1/2 teaspoon garam masala

2 tomatoes, chopped

6 green cardamon pods (use only the seeds)

1/2 teaspoon salt, or to taste

3 cups water

*To make the koftas:*

1) If using lotus root: Dry lotus root must be soaked in water *overnight*. Peel and cut the lotus root into small pieces. Soak in salted water. Then wash thoroughly and boil or steam until tender. Drain off the water and mash.

If using potatoes: Boil or steam the potatoes until tender. Remove from the water, peel and mash.

2) To the mashed vegetables, add the green chiles, chickpea flour, garam masala, cumin powder, coriander leaves and crushed almonds. Add ¼ of the mashed panir. Mix well and add turmeric to color the mixture yellow.

3) With this mixture, make small balls the size of a walnut. Then cover these balls with a layer of the uncolored panir and form into egg shapes. Then cover these "eggs" with another layer of the yellow mixture.

4) In a thick-bottomed saucepan, heat the 2 cups of vegetable oil or ghee and carefully immerse the "eggs" into the hot oil, deep frying until brown. Remove with a slotted spoon, letting the excess oil drip back into the pan. Drain further on paper towels.

*For the curry sauce:*
1) In a thick-bottomed frying pan or wok, heat the 3 teaspoons of oil or ghee and saute the onions until transparent. Add the garlic, ginger and 1 cup of water. Cook until the water is completely evaporated.

2) Add the red chiles, garam masala, tomatoes, green cardamon and salt. Continue to cook, stirring continuously, until the oil starts to separate out. Then add 3 cups of water and cook until it becomes a soupy gravy.

*To serve:*
1) Cut the "eggs" in half, the long way. Arrange on a platter and pour the curry sauce over them.

Yield: 8-10 "eggs" and 1 cup sauce

# Lotus Root Koftas with Mushrooms
## (Kanwal Kakree ee Khumbaa)

Really delicious, with a meaty texture!

For the lotus root koftas:
1 pound lotus root (4 or 5 six-inch-long roots)
1/2 teaspoon white cumin powder
1/4 teaspoon black cardamon powder
1 teaspoon cinnamon powder

---

2 teaspoons vegetable oil or ghee for frying
8 teaspoons chickpea (garbanzo) flour

---

1 teaspoon fresh ginger, peeled and finely chopped
4 green cardamon pods (use only the seeds)
1 teaspoon red chile powder
1/2 teaspoon garam masala
1 teaspoon cumin seeds
1 teaspoon fresh coriander leaves, chopped
1/2 teaspoon salt, or to taste

---

1 pound mushrooms (about 36 medium-sized mushrooms)
1/4 cup unbleached white flour for dusting

---

2 cups vegetable oil or ghee for deep frying

---

For the curry sauce:
2 teaspoons vegetable oil or ghee for frying
1 cup onions, chopped
8 cloves garlic, chopped
2 teaspoons fresh ginger, peeled and finely chopped

---

1 cup water
1/4 teaspoon crushed dry red chiles
1 tomato, peeled and chopped
3 green cardamon pods (use only the seeds)
1/2 teaspoon white cumin seeds
1/2 teaspoon garam masala
1/4 teaspoon salt, or to taste
1/2 cup yogurt

---

2 tablespoons coriander leaves

*To make the lotus root koftas:*
1) If the lotus root is dry, soak in water *overnight*.

2) Peel the lotus root and cut into small pieces. Soak these in salted water for 15 minutes, then drain off the water and wash thoroughly. Boil the lotus root in water with the white cumin powder, black cardamon powder and cinnamon. When the lotus root is tender, strain off the liquid and mash the lotus root. Set aside.

3) In a thick-bottomed frying pan, heat the 2 tablespoons of vegetable oil or ghee and fry the chickpea (garbanzo) flour until light brown. Remove immediately from the heat.

4) To the mashed lotus root add 1 teaspoon ginger, seeds of 4 green cardamon pods, 1 teaspoon chile powder, 1 teaspoon garam masala, 1 teaspoon cumin seeds, 1 teaspoon coriander leaves, ½ teaspoon salt and the fried flour. Blend it all together until it forms a thick paste.

5) With this paste, form small balls about the size of a walnut. With your thumb, make an indentation in each ball. Fill this with chopped mushrooms and seal it with some more lotus root paste. Set the remaining mushrooms aside for use later. Roll the balls in the unbleached white flour.

6) In a thick-bottomed saucepan or wok, heat the 2 cups of oil or ghee and deep fry the balls over a low heat until light brown. Remove with a slotted spoon, letting the excess oil drip back into the pan. Set aside.


*To make the curry sauce:*
1) In a large, thick-bottomed frying pan, heat the 2 teaspoons of vegetable oil or ghee and saute the onions, garlic and 2 teaspoons of ginger until light brown. Then add 1 cup of water, ¼ teaspoon red chiles, tomatoes, seeds of 3 cardamon pods, cumin seeds, ⅓ teaspoon of garam masala, ¼ teaspoon salt and yogurt. Stir continuously and cook until all the liquid is absorbed and the oil starts to separate out. Then add the remaining mushrooms, stirring frequently to prevent sticking. Cook until the mushrooms are done.

2) Ten minutes before serving, add the deep fried balls to the curry and cook on a low heat, stirring very gently, until the curry has saturated the balls. Sprinkle with 2 tablespoons of coriander leaves before serving.

Yield: 12 balls and 2½ cups sauce

# Deep Fried Panir in Curry Sauce
## (Paneer Koftaa Karee)

Serve with plain rice and a sweet chutney.

2 tablespoons unbleached
  white flour
¼ teaspoon salt, or to taste

enough water to make a thin
  batter

---

1 cup panir, cut into cubes
  (see recipe p. 24)

---

2 cups vegetable oil or ghee
  for deep frying

---

¼ cup vegetable oil or ghee
  for sauteing
2 medium onions, chopped
6 cloves garlic, chopped

1 tablespoon fresh ginger,
  peeled and finely chopped
4 green chiles, mild or hot, to
  taste, chopped

---

½ teaspoon red chile powder
1 teaspoon turmeric
½ teaspoon salt, or to taste
1 teaspoon cumin powder
1 teaspoon poppy seeds
4 whole cloves

4 green cardamon pods (use
  only the seeds)
12 almonds, peeled and
  chopped fine
2 tablespoons water

---

½ cup yogurt

enough water to make sauce

---

1 tablespoon fresh coriander
  or mint leaves, chopped

100

1) In a bowl, sift together the flour and ¼ teaspoon of salt and add enough water to make a thin batter.

2) Dip the panir cubes in the batter.

3) In a thick-bottomed saucepan, heat the 2 cups of vegetable oil or ghee for deep frying, and deep fry the coated panir cubes until light brown. Remove with a slotted spoon, letting the excess oil drip back into the pan. Drain further on paper towels.

4) In a large, thick-bottomed frying pan or wok, heat the ¼ cup of vegetable oil or ghee and saute the onions, garlic, ginger and green chiles until golden brown. Then add the red chile powder, turmeric, salt, cumin powder, poppy seeds, cloves, green cardamon and almonds. (Peel the almonds by immersing in boiling water for a few minutes; the skins can then be "pinched" off.) Stir well, add 2 tablespoons of water, and fry until the oil starts to separate out.

5) Add the yogurt and simmer for a few minutes, stirring continuously. Add enough water to make a soupy sauce and cook 5 more minutes.

6) Add the deep fried panir. Continue cooking on a low heat for 5 minutes. Remove from the heat, sprinkle with chopped coriander or mint leaves and serve.

Yield: 16 cubes panir and 4 cups sauce

# Banana Kofta Curry
## (Kelaa Koftaa)

An excellent dish with a most unusual taste.

For the koftas:
4 unripe bananas

1 inch piece fresh ginger,
  peeled and chopped fine
1 medium onion, chopped
  fine

1/2 teaspoon salt, or to taste
juice of 1 lemon
3 tablespoons mild cheese,
  grated

2 cups vegetable oil or ghee
  for deep frying

For the curry sauce:
1/4 vegetable oil or ghee for
  sauteing
2 medium onions, chopped

6 cloves garlic, chopped
1 teaspoon fresh ginger,
  peeled and finely chopped

2 medium tomatoes, chopped
4 green chiles, mild or hot, to
  taste, chopped fine
1 teaspoon turmeric

1/2 teaspoon red chile powder
1/2 teaspoon salt, or to taste
enough water to make a sauce

1 cup cream

For the garnish:
a few fresh coriander leaves

a pinch of garam masala

*To make the koftas:*
1) Peel the bananas, steam until soft and mash.

2) Grind the ginger and onions together. Add the salt, lemon juice, grated cheese and banana. Mix thoroughly to form a thick paste.

3) Form this mixture into small balls, about the size of a walnut. In a thick-bottomed saucepan or wok, heat the 2 cups of oil or ghee for deep frying and deep fry the banana balls on a medium heat until golden brown. Remove with a slotted spoon, letting the excess oil drip back into the pan. Set aside.

*To make the curry:*
1) In a large, thick-bottomed frying pan, heat the vegetable oil or ghee and saute the onions, garlic and ginger until golden brown.

2) Add the tomatoes, green chiles, turmeric, red chile powder and salt. Mix well and simmer for a few minutes. When the tomatoes get mushy and the oil starts to separate out, add enough water to make a sauce. Boil for 5 minutes.

3) Turn off the heat. In a bowl, beat the cream a little to thicken it, but not till it foams, then add to curry sauce, mixing well. Place the banana balls in a flat casserole. Pour the sauce on top of the balls but do not stir. Place the casserole, covered, in a warm oven until ready to serve. Before serving, garnish with fresh coriander leaves and a sprinkle of garam masala.

Yield: 5-6 cups

# Stuffed Potato Bhujia

The sauce makes this fancy party dish taste just divine!

For the potatoes:
*3 medium potatoes*  *3 teaspoons butter or ghee*
*3/4 teaspoon salt, or to taste*

For the filling:
*panir from 1 quart of milk (see* *1 tablespoon peeled fresh*
   *recipe p. 24)*    *ginger, finely chopped*
*2 tablespoons raisins*  *a few, fresh coriander leaves*
*1 green chile, mild or hot, to*  *1/2 teaspoon salt, or to taste*
   *taste, chopped*  *2 tablespoons tomato sauce*
*1 tablespoon cumin powder*

For the baking:
*unbleached flour for dusting*  *4 tablespoons vegetable oil or*
   *potatoes*    *ghee for baking*

For the frying:
*1/2 tablespoon ghee*  *1/2 teaspoon asafoetida*
*1/2 tablespoon white flour*  *1 1/2 cups yogurt*

*2 teaspoons cumin powder*  *3/4 teaspoon red chile powder,*
*1 teaspoon garam masala*    *mild or hot, to taste*
*1 teaspoon ginger*  *a few, fresh coriander leaves*

*1/4 teaspoon salt, or to taste*  *1 tomato, chopped*

Garnish:
*a few more coriander leaves*

1) Bake the potatoes until tender. Cut them in half and scoop out the insides. Mash the potato pulp, 1/4 teaspoon salt and 3 teaspoons butter or ghee and set aside.

2) Mix together the filling ingredients: panir, raisins, green chiles, cumin powder, ginger, coriander leaves, 1/2 teaspoon salt and 2 tablespoons of tomato sauce.

3) Baking: Half fill the hollow potatoes with this mixture. Then finish filling the potatoes with the mashed potatoes. Lightly dust the filled potatoes with flour. Oil a baking pan with 4 tablespoons oil or ghee. Place potatoes on pan and bake at 350 degrees till warmed through (10-15 minutes).

4) Frying: Now heat ½ tablespoon of ghee and fry ½ tablespoon white flour, ½ teaspoon of asafoetida water and the yogurt. Add the 2 teaspoons of cumin, garam masala, 1 teaspoon ginger, red chile powder and a few coriander leaves. Fry for a few minutes. Add ¼ teaspoon of salt and chopped tomatoes and continue to cook for a few minutes. Serve on top of potatoes as a sauce.

5) Garnish: Before serving, sprinkle with a few more coriander leaves.

Yield: 6 stuffed potato halves

# Stuffed Bell Pepper
## (Simlaa Mirach Bujiaa)

6 medium bell peppers (sweet
   green peppers)

| | |
|---|---|
| 4 medium potatoes<br>½ pound (about 1½ cups)<br>   green peas, fresh or frozen | salted water for boiling<br>   potatoes and peas |
| 3 tablespoons vegetable oil or<br>   ghee for frying<br>1 Spanish onion, chopped<br>   fine | 1 teaspoon fresh ginger,<br>   peeled and finely chopped |
| ¼ teaspoon turmeric<br>¼ teaspoon red chile powder<br>¼ teaspoon mango powder<br>½ teaspoon garam masala | ½ teaspoon salt, or to taste<br>¼ teaspoon pomegranate<br>   seeds |

4 tablespoons vegetable oil or
   ghee for baking

1) Wash the bell peppers and dip them in boiling water for 1 minute. They will become crisper and lighter in color. Carefully remove from the water, drain and cool.

2) Peel the potatoes and cut into small cubes. Boil the potatoes and peas together in salted water, using as little water as possible. When they are cooked, drain off any left-over water and mash the vegetables together.

3) In a large, thick-bottomed frying pan, heat 3 tablespoons of vegetable oil or ghee and fry the onions and ginger until golden brown. Add the turmeric, chile powder, mango powder, garam masala, ½ teaspoon salt and pomegranate seeds, and mix well. Then add the mashed vegetables, stir thoroughly, and fry for a few more minutes. Remove from the heat.

4) Carefully cut off the stems of the peppers and scoop out the seeds. Stuff each pepper with the vegetable mixture. Tie a thread around each pepper so the stuffing cannot fall out during cooking.

5) Oil a baking pan with 4 tablespoons oil or ghee and place the peppers on it. Bake the peppers at 350 degrees until they begin to brown (about 40 minutes). Remove from the oven, snip off the threads and serve.

Yield: 6 stuffed peppers

# Stuffed Bitter Melon
## (Karelaa Masaalewaalaa)

2-3 medium-sized bitter
  melons

a pinch or two of salt to
  sprinkle on melons

---

2 tablespoons pomegranate
  seeds or mango powder
3 medium onions, chopped
  very fine
1 teaspoon red chile powder,
  mild or hot, to taste

1 teaspoon turmeric
1 teaspoon garam masala
1 teaspoon salt, or to taste
¼ cup vegetable oil or ghee
  for frying (optional)

---

3 tablespoons vegetable oil or
  ghee for baking

1) To prepare the bitter melons: Peel and scrape the bitter melons and cut lengthwise. Remove the seeds. Sprinkle the melons with salt, place in a bowl, and set aside for *1 hour.* Then thoroughly wash the melons so that the salt and bitterness is washed out. Squeeze them gently with your hands to remove all excess liquid.

2) Grind the pomegranate seeds and mix with the onions, chile powder, turmeric, garam masala and salt. (Optional: saute these ingredients in vegetable oil or ghee before continuing with step 3.)

3) Stuff the bitter melons with this mixture. Tie the melons with threads so the stuffing cannot fall out during cooking.

4) Oil a baking pan with 3 tablespoons oil or ghee and place melons on it. Bake the melons at 350 degrees until they begin to brown (about 40 minutes). Remove from the oven, snip off the threads and serve.

Yield: 2 or 3 stuffed melons

# Stuffed Cabbage
## (Masaalewaalee Band Gobee)

This is a lightly spiced, satisfying side dish for special occasions.

| | |
|---|---|
| 1 large cabbage | salted water for blanching cabbage leaves |

24 large potatoes

| | |
|---|---|
| ¼ cup vegetable oil or ghee for frying | 2 large green chiles, mild or hot, to taste, chopped fine |
| 2 large onions, chopped | 1 bunch fresh coriander leaves |
| 4 cloves garlic, chopped | |
| 1 inch piece fresh ginger, peeled and chopped fine | |

| | |
|---|---|
| ½ teaspoon chile powder, or to taste | 1 teaspoon turmeric |
| ½ teaspoon garam masala | ½ teaspoon salt, or to taste |

1 lemon

1) To prepare the cabbage leaves for rolling: In boiling salted water, blanch the cabbage leaves (2 at a time) for 4-5 minutes, until leaves but not stems soften, but not till leaves change color. Remove from the water, drain, cover with a towel to prevent drying, and set aside to cool.

2) While you are blanching batches of leaves, boil the potatoes until tender, peel and cut into small pieces.

3) In a large, thick-bottomed frying pan or wok, heat the oil or ghee and fry the onions, garlic, ginger, green chiles and coriander until the onions are golden brown.

4) Add the chile powder, garam masala, turmeric, salt and the potatoes. Continue to fry for 3 minutes, stirring frequently.

5) Remove from the heat, sprinkle with the juice of 1 lemon, mix well, and set aside to cool.

6) Remove the hard stems from the blanched cabbage leaves and spread the leaves out on a flat surface. Put a portion of the potato mixture at the edge of a leaf, gently turn the sides of the leaf inward and roll up the mixture in the leaf. (If the leaves are small, lay 2 leaves overlapping each other and roll as one.) Serve hot.

Yield: 15-20 stuffed leaves

# The Holy Man and the Dog

Once there was an old holy man who was noted for his humility. He would sit by the side of the road singing songs of praise to God. Trusting in God to provide for all his needs, he would eat only what was offered to him. When people brought him a morsel or two of food, he would thank them in the name of his Creator and pray for them.

Although he was very well loved and respected, he would sometimes go for several days with barely a piece of bread to eat and a glass of water to drink. People would pass by and, seeing him by the roadside singing his simple songs in utter contentment and absorption, forget that perhaps he was hungry.

On just such a day, at the end of a week of hungry days, the old man was blessed by the generosity of a young woman. It being her birthday, she had cooked much delicious food for distribution to the poor and the needy in thankfulness for being given the gift of life. When she came to the holy man's spot, she bowed before him and touched his feet. Then she set before him a bag of steaming fresh chapatis and a container of ghee to spread upon them. He smiled and blessed her, and then, with the welcome aroma of fried whole wheat filling his nostrils, began afresh his song of praise.

As the holy man was rising from his spot to begin his walk home, his bag of chapatis in one hand, the ghee in the other, a stray dog of the village came tearing down the road. As it ran by the old man, it tore the bag of chapatis from his hand and made off with them at full speed. The old man, without skipping a beat, took off after him. "Come back, come back," he cried, "those chapatis are dry! Here, have some ghee. It will make them more tasty!"

A travelling merchant who had observed the scene remarked to his companion, "Who was that old man who came running by?" "That was no man," his friend replied, "for no man could care so much more about a stray dog than about his own well-being. That 'old man' we just saw was God Himself."

# Breads

In the villages of northern India, round, thin, unleavened, whole wheat breads are not only the basic food but the primary eating utensil as well. Since almost all vegetarian preparations are either creamy or in small pieces, there is no need for knives. And because of the chapati and thousands of years of practice, forks are obsolete. One simply breaks off a piece of bread, folds it around a bit of food, and scoops it up into one's mouth. And because of traditional hygienic prohibitions, this is all done using only the right hand!

According to yogic philosophy, eating with the hands actually increases the nourishment derived from the food. It is believed that ambient energy (prana) is absorbed directly from the food into the body through the hands. Certainly, this is the method of eating which young children enjoy the most!

For the unpracticed Westerner who does not wish to delve too deeply into Indian culture, Indian breads serve simply as light, delicious, fresh accompaniments to a meal. When filled with vegetables and fried, they can serve as a light meal by themselves.

In the traditional society of India, the woman of the house cooks the meal, and while her family sits down to eat, she continues on in the kitchen turning out light, fluffy, fresh breads, one after another, as many as anyone can eat. Only after the family is completely satisfied will she settle down to her own meal. This is the ideal way to eat Indian breads, made and served with such selfless devotion and love, hot off the griddle.

Of course, this is not the way that most Westerners choose to express their family ties. The whole family wants to sit down and eat together. As an alternative, these breads can be made just before the meal, stacked in a bowl lined with a clean cloth, covered, and kept warming in the oven. The cloth absorbs the steam rising off the fresh breads and thus keeps them from becoming soggy.

# Some Advice for
# Successful Indian Bread Making

## Utensils

You will need these utensils for making Indian breads:

a bowl for mixing dough

a pastry board or flat surface for kneading and rolling out the dough

a large, heavy, smooth-surfaced, cast-iron frying pan or griddle for cooking the breads

a heavy, deep, cast-iron frying pan or wok for deep frying

a rolling pin

a stainless steel slotted spoon or spatula

a pair of tongs

cloth napkins or dish towels

paper towels

## Flour

The flour used in most Indian breads is whole wheat *pastry* flour. Pastry flour is a finer grind of flour than regular whole wheat flour, with most of the coarse bran flakes ground down. This gives the flour a silky texture especially suited to making soft, smooth unleavened bread.

If you are unable to get whole wheat pastry flour, you can use the whole wheat flour available in the supermarket, but adjust it by either: (1) sifting it through a fine-meshed sieve to remove the larger flakes of bran (you can save these and sprinkle them on cereal), or (2) mixing it with unbleached white all-purpose flour in a ratio of 2 cups of whole wheat flour to one cup of white all-purpose flour *or* half and half, depending on which mixture best makes the bread you like.

Even better than the whole wheat pastry flour or the blend, however, is a flour made especially for Indian breads. It is available in Indian and some West Indian groceries. It's called *aattaa* and is marketed under the name "Chapati Flour."

## Serving and Storing

If you want to make a large quantity of chapatis so you don't have to make them fresh each meal, you can cook them on only one side, take them off the griddle, let them cool, and then put them in the refrigerator or the freezer. When you next want to eat them, just dampen the uncooked side with a little water and put it in the oven at 400 degrees or on broil. The wet side will be facing up. Very soon the chapati will be soft and a little browned and hot to eat. Just spread with a little butter or ghee.

And if you're traveling and want to take chapatis with you, instead of using water in the dough, use milk. These chapatis stay so soft that they'll keep fresh tasting for a couple of days. Even better for traveling or for lunch boxes are stuffed pranthas. They stay fresh and get even more delicious after a couple of days.

# Chapati
## (Chapaatee)

2 cups (approximately) whole wheat pastry flour or chapati flour

1 cup water (enough to make a bread dough consistency)

1/2 cup whole wheat pastry (or chapati) flour in a small bowl (optional)

2 tablespoons (approximately) ghee or butter for spreading

To make the dough:

1) Place the 2 cups of flour in a bowl. Make a well in the center. Add the water into the well, gradually mixing the flour into the water to form a soft dough. Mix until a compact mass is formed. If the dough is too crumbly, add a little more water.

2) Place the dough on a flat surface and knead it for 5 minutes, until the dough is soft and smooth and pliable. Add a little flour if needed to keep dough from sticking to surface. Then put the dough back into a bowl, cover with a slightly damp cloth and let it rest for 15-20 minutes.

*To make the chapati:*
1) Knead the dough a few more times.

2) Break off a piece of dough and roll it between your palms to form a small ball about 1½ inches in diameter. (See figure 1).

3) Place the dough ball on a lightly floured pastry board or flat surface for rolling. (Optional; roll the dough ball into the small bowl of flour instead of flouring the board.) Using a rolling pin, roll into a circle about 6 to 9 inches in diameter, 1/8 inch thick. (See figure 2).

*To cook the chapati:*
1) Carefully lift the chapati and place it onto a hot griddle or iron frying pan. Bake until the top surface starts to form little bubbles (about 20 to 30 seconds). Immediately flip it over with a pair of tongs or a spatula and cook the other side until it browns (8 to 10 seconds).

Figure 1

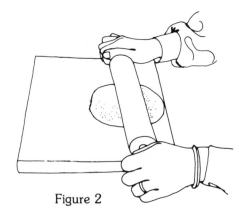

Figure 2

If you are cooking on a gas stove, you may get best results by first placing the chapati directly on a burner over a medium flame.

2) Then, using a clean cloth or napkin, press it gently in the center. The chapati should puff up like a balloon. (See figure 3.) When it puffs up like that it is known as a "phulka." (See figure 3.)

3) Place the cooked chapati on a clean cloth and spread lightly with ghee or butter.

4) Clean excess flour off griddle after cooking each chapati.

5) Serve hot!

Yield: 6 chapatis

Figure 3

# Plain Pranthas
## (Paraanthaa)

1 cup whole wheat pastry
  flour or chapati flour
1/2 teaspoon salt (optional)
1/2 cup water
1/2 cup whole wheat pastry or
  chapati flour in small bowl
  (optional)

1/4 cup (approximately) ghee
or butter for spreading

*To make the dough:*
1) Place the flour and salt in a bowl. Make a well in the center. Add the water into the well gradually, mixing the flour into the water to form a soft dough. Mix until a compact mass of dough is formed.

2) Place the dough on a flat surface and knead for 5 minutes, until the dough is soft and smooth and pliable. Then put the dough back into a bowl, cover with a slightly damp cloth, and let it rest for 15 to 20 minutes.

*To make the pranthas:*
1) Knead the rested dough a few more times.

2) Break off a piece of dough and roll it between your hands to make a small ball about 1½ inches in diameter.

3) Place the dough ball onto a lightly floured pastry board (or roll in bowl of flour and use unfloured surface). Using a rolling pin, roll into a circle about 5 inches in diameter, 1/8 inch thick.

4) Lightly spread ghee or butter on the raw circle, fold it in half, and then spread the upper surface with more butter or ghee. Fold it again, either in half or in thirds, and roll it into a ball again. Lightly flour dough ball, if necessary, and roll the dough out again into a circle about 5 inches in diameter, 1/8 inch thick.

*To bake the prantha:*
1) Carefully place a prantha onto a hot griddle or iron frying pan. Bake until the top surface starts to form little bubbles (about 20 to

30 seconds). Immediately flip it over to brown on the other side (for about 8 to 10 seconds).

2) When both sides are cooked, spread 1 teaspoon of ghee or butter on each side, and fry each side once more until golden brown. Serve hot.

3) Clean excess flour off griddle after cooking each prantha.

Yield: 4 pranthas

# Stuffed Pranthas
## ("Stuffed" Paraanthaa)

For the dough:
1 cup whole wheat pastry
   flour
1/2 teaspoon salt (optional)
1/2 cup water

1/2 cup whole wheat pastry or
   chapati flour in small bowl
   (optional)

---

For the filling:
2 teaspoons green chiles, mild
   or hot, to taste, chopped
1 medium onion, grated
1 pound (about 3 1/4 cups)
   vegetables, finely grated
   (white radishes, cauliflower,
   carrots) or boiled and
   mashed potatoes. This is
   equivalent to 2 medium
   potatoes, 4 medium carrots,
   or 1/2 large cauliflower.

2 tablespoons fresh ginger,
   peeled and finely chopped
1 teaspoon oregano or celery
   seeds
1 teaspoon garlic powder
1 teaspoon red chile powder
   or ground black pepper
1/2 teaspoon salt, or to taste

---

1/2 cup (approximately) ghee
   or butter for spreading

*To make the dough:*
Follow the directions in the previous recipe. (See "Pranthas.")

117

*To make the filling:*
Mix together the green chiles, onion, vegetables, ginger, oregano or celery seeds, garlic, red chile or black pepper and salt. Squeeze them in your hands until all the liquid comes out and the mixture is very dry.

Figure 4

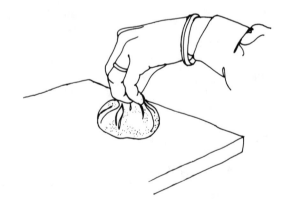

Figure 5

*To make the stuffed prantha (Method I):*
1) Knead the dough a few more times.

2) Break off a piece of dough and roll it between your palms to make a small ball about 1½ inches in diameter. (See figure 1).

3) Place the dough ball onto a lightly floured pastry board (or roll in bowl of flour and use unfloured surface). Using a rolling pin, roll into a small thick circle about 3 to 6 inches in diameter.

4) Place a portion of the filling into the center of the circle. (See figure 4). Fold over the sides of the dough to cover the filling. (See figure 5). (If the dough breaks while folding, repair by placing a little piece of dough over the hole.)

5) Place the filled dough onto a lightly floured pastry board or flat surface for rolling. Using a rolling pin, carefully roll out into a circle about 5 inches in diameter, 1/8 inch thick.

*To make the stuffed prantha (Method II):*
1) Prepare the dough as above.

2) Roll out into 2 small chapatis.

3) Place a portion of the filling on one chapati. Cover it with the other chapati.

4) Flatten this "sandwich" with your hands. Then place it on a lightly floured pastry board or flat surface and roll out carefully with a rolling pin.

*To bake the stuffed prantha:*
1) Carefully place the stuffed prantha onto a hot griddle or iron frying pan. Cook for 1 minute on each side.

2) Then spread 1 tablespoon of ghee or butter on each side of the prantha and fry each side until crisp and golden brown.

3) When both sides are cooked, spread again with ghee or butter. Serve hot with yogurt.

Yield: 3 stuffed pranthas

# Pathuras
## *(Pathuraa)*

Serve these thick, bland pancakes with a salty condiment.

*2 medium potatoes, grated*
*2½ cups unbleached white*
*  flour (approximately;*
*  enough to hold the potatoes*
*  together into a dough)*

*1 teaspoon salt, or to taste*
*½ cup white flour in a small*
*  bowl (optional)*
*2 cups vegetable oil or ghee*
*  for deep frying*

*To make the dough:*
Grate the raw potatoes into a bowl. Add enough flour and salt to form a dough. Mix well. (No water is necessary, since the potatoes have enough water in them to hold the mixture together.) Let the dough rest in a warm place for ½ hour only.

*To make the pathura:*
1) Break off a piece of dough and roll it between your palms to form a small ball about 1½ inches in diameter.

2) Place the dough ball on a lightly floured pastry board (or roll in bowl of flour and use unfloured surface). Using a rolling pin, roll into a circle like a small chapati.

3) In a deep, thick-bottomed frying pan or wok, heat the oil or ghee to smoking point.

4) Carefully immerse the pathura into the hot oil or ghee and deep fry until golden brown.

5) Remove from the oil with a slotted spoon, letting the excess oil drip back into the pan. Serve hot with chutney.

Yield: 15 pathuras

# Puris
## (Pooree)

2 cups whole wheat pastry
   flour or chapati flour
½ cup water
2 cups ghee or vegetable oil
   (for deep frying)

2 cups whole wheat pastry or
   chapati flour in a small bowl
   (optional)

*To make the dough:*
Use directions for "Chapati." (See p. 113)

*To make the puri:*
1) Knead the dough a few more times.

2) Break off a piece of dough and roll it between your palms to form a small ball about 1 inch in diameter.

3) Place the dough ball onto a lightly floured pastry board or flat surface for rolling (or roll in small bowl of flour and use an unfloured board). Using a rolling pin, roll out into a circle about 3 inches in diameter, 1/8 inch thick.

*To cook the puri:*
1) In a deep, thick-bottomed saucepan, heat the vegetable oil or ghee to smoking point.

2) Immerse the raw puri in the oil or ghee and press down lightly in the center with a flat spoon. When the puri floats back up to the surface and puffs up like a balloon, carefully turn it over with a spoon. Fry until it is golden brown. Then remove the puri with a slotted spoon, letting the excess oil drip back into the pan. Place the cooked puri on a paper towel to remove any extra oil.

3) Serve very hot with any curry or with honey.

Yield: 10-12 puris

# Stuffed Puris

## (Masaalewaalee Pooree)

For the yeast for the dough:

| | |
|---|---|
| 1/2 cup unbleached white flour | 1/4 teaspoon baking soda |
| 2 teaspoons yogurt | 1/2-3/4 cup lukewarm water |

Other prep:

| | |
|---|---|
| 1 cup split black mung beans, washed well | 4 cups water |

For the dough:

| | |
|---|---|
| 2 1/2 cups (approximately) unbleached white flour | 1/2-3/4 cups lukewarm water |

For the filling:

| | |
|---|---|
| 2 teaspoons red chile powder | 4 cups water |
| 2 teaspoons garam masala | 1/4 cup vegetable oil or ghee for sauteing |
| 1/2 teaspoon salt, or to taste | |

2 cups vegetable oil or ghee
   for deep frying

*To make the yeast for the dough:*
1) Mix the unbleached white flour, yogurt, baking soda and lukewarm water together in a bowl and *keep it in a warm place for at least 24 hours* (in winter, keep it for 2 days).

*Other preparation:*
Soak the split black mung beans in water *overnight*.

*To make the dough:*
1) Place the flour in a bowl and make a well in the center. Gradually add the yeast and lukewarm water into the well, mixing the flour in to form a soft dough. Mix until a compact ball of dough is formed.

2) Place the dough on a flat surface and knead for 5 minutes, adding flour to keep dough from sticking to surface. Put the dough back into a bowl, sprinkle the top with a little water and oil, and cover with a slightly damp cloth. *Let the dough rise until it doubles in size* (about 1 1/2 hours).

*To make the filling:*
Drain the water off the mung beans (which have been soaked overnight). Blend the beans in a blender until a thick paste is formed. Add the chile powder, garam masala, salt and 4 cups of water and mix well. In a thick-bottomed frying pan, heat ¼ cup oil or ghee and saute this paste until the beans stick together in one mass and separate from the sides of the pan (about 20 minutes). Set aside to cool.

*To make the stuffed puri:*
1) Punch down the dough, kneading it again with a little water added to keep it pliable.

2) Break off a piece of dough and, with wet hands, form it into a small ball about 1½ inches in diameter.

3) Place the dough ball onto a lightly floured pastry board or flat surface for rolling. Using a rolling pin, roll out halfway. Place about 2 tablespoons of the bean filling in the center and fold the sides of the dough up over the filling.

4) Using your hands, carefully press the filled ball into a puri-sized pancake about 3 inches in diameter.

*To cook the stuffed puri:*
1) In a deep, thick-bottomed frying pan or wok, heat the 2 cups of vegetable oil or ghee.

2) Carefully immerse the raw stuffed puri into the oil or ghee and press down very lightly in the center with a flat spoon. When the puri floats back up to the surface and puffs up like a balloon, carefully turn it over with the spoon. Fry it until it is golden brown. Then remove the puri with a slotted spoon, letting the excess oil drip back into the pan. Place the cooked puri on a clean cloth or napkin to remove any extra oil. Serve very hot.

Yield: 20 stuffed puris

# Rice Dishes

In south and east India, rice (*chaawal*) is almost as essential to eating as chewing; every mouthful of food is usually accompanied by a bite of rice. The rice serves as a filling and coarsely textured contrast to the spicier and saucier vegetable or bean dishes. In the north, where wheat is more plentiful, bread serves much the same purpose.

India produces more than one thousand varieties of rice. The rice I recommend for my recipes is basmati rice, a long-grained, white, slightly nutty-tasting rice. It is available in all Indian food stores and some natural food stores. There is also a rice marketed in the western and southwestern United States which is similar in taste to basmati rice. It's grown in Texas and called, appropriately, Texmati rice. Texmati rice tends to break up into smaller grains while cooking, which will give a different texture to the dishes.

Rice complements most dishes which are soupy or made with gravy.

# Plain Fried Rice
## *(Chaawal)*

2 cups rice

---

4 tablespoons vegetable oil or
  ghee
2 medium onions, chopped

6 cloves garlic, chopped
2 tablespoons fresh ginger,
  peeled and finely chopped

---

4 whole cloves
1 small cinnamon stick
6 black peppercorns
4 green cardamon pods (use
  only the seeds)

¾ teaspoon salt, or to taste
4 cups water

1) Carefully wash and drain the rice.

2) In a large, thick-bottomed pot, heat the vegetable oil or ghee and fry the onion, garlic and ginger until golden brown. Add the cloves, cinnamon, black peppercorns, cardamon and salt and fry for 1 more minute. Add the rice, stir and fry for 2 minutes more. Then add the water, cover and bring to a boil. Immediately turn down the heat and simmer until the rice is tender and the water is absorbed.

3) Turn off the heat, keep covered and let sit for 5 minutes. Serve with a curry, yogurt or raita.

Yield: 4½ cups

# Vegetable Rice
## (Biryaanee)

| | |
|---|---|
| 1/2 cup ghee | 1/2 cup panir, cubed (see recipe p. 24) |

| | |
|---|---|
| 1 large onion, chopped | 2 teaspoons crushed red chiles |
| 3 whole cloves | 1 small cinnamon stick |
| 2 teaspoons cumin powder | 2 1/2 teaspoons salt |
| 4 green cardamon pods (use only the seeds) | |

| | |
|---|---|
| 1 cup green peas, fresh or frozen | 2 tablespoons almonds, soaked and peeled |
| 1 large carrot, chopped | 4 cups water |

| | |
|---|---|
| 2 cups rice | 1 bay leaf |
| 1 cup milk | |

Optional garnish:

| | |
|---|---|
| 1/4 teaspoon kewra essence | 2 silver leaves |

1) In a large, thick-bottomed pot, heat the vegetable oil or ghee and fry the panir cubes until they are light brown. Then remove them and set aside.

2) In this oil, fry the onions until light brown. Then add the cloves, cumin, cardamon seeds, red chiles, cinnamon and salt and stir well, continuing to fry until the onions are brown. Add the peas, carrots, almonds and fried panir and fry a few more minutes. Add the water and bring to a boil.

3) Wash the rice thoroughly and drain. Add the rice, milk and bay leaf to the boiling mixture and let it come to a boil again. Then cover, reduce to low heat, and cook until the rice is tender and all the liquid is absorbed.

4) Keep covered, remove from the heat, and let sit for 10 minutes. Before serving, remove cinnamon stick and (optional) sprinkle with kewra essence and decorate with silver leaf.

Yield: 10 cups

# Mixed Vegetable Rice
## (Pilaao)

A mild side dish. Complement with a spicy vegetable or bean dish.

### RECIPE I

| | |
|---|---|
| 2 cups rice | 4 cups water |

| | |
|---|---|
| 4 tablespoons vegetable oil or ghee | 1 small cinnamon stick |
| 1 teaspoon cumin seeds | 8 whole black peppercorns |
| 6 whole cloves | 1 teaspoon salt, or to taste |

| | |
|---|---|
| 1 cup green peas, fresh or frozen | 1 cup string beans, chopped |
| 1 cup carrots, peeled and sliced thin | 1 cup cauliflower, cut into small pieces |

### RECIPE II

As in Recipe I, plus:

| | |
|---|---|
| 2 medium onions, chopped | 2 tablespoons fresh ginger, peeled and finely chopped |
| 6 cloves garlic, chopped | |

### RECIPE I

1) Carefully wash and drain the rice. In a large, thick-bottomed pot, bring 4 cups of water to a boil, add the rice and let it come to a boil again. Then lower the heat and simmer until the rice is tender and all the water is absorbed. Remove from the heat.

2) In a large, thick-bottomed frying pan, heat the vegetable oil or ghee and add the cumin, cloves, cinnamon, black peppercorns and salt and stir well. Lower the heat and add the peas, carrots, string beans and cauliflower. Cover for 5 minutes.

3) Then add the vegetable/spice mixture to the cooked rice, stir well, and keep on a low heat for 3 minutes. Fluff up with a fork and remove the cinnamon stick before serving.

RECIPE II

1) Carefully wash and drain the rice.

2) In a large, thick-bottomed frying pan or wok, heat the vegetable oil or ghee and fry the onions, garlic and ginger until golden brown. Add the green peas, carrots, string beans and cauliflower and stir well. Reduce to a low heat and cover the pan for 5 minutes.

3) Add the cumin, cloves, cinnamon, black peppercorns and salt and fry for 1 minute. Add the rice and fry, stirring continuously, for 1 minute. Then add the water, bring to a boil, cover, and cook on a low heat until the rice is tender and all the water absorbed. Turn off the heat, but keep the pan covered for 5 more minutes. Remove the cinnamon stick and serve with plain yogurt.

Yield: about 8 cups

# Sweet Yellow Rice
## (Zardaa Pilaao)

A fancy dish for formal occasions. Very sweet.

1 cup rice

---

1/3 cup water
1/3 cup honey

a pinch of saffron (for color)

---

2 tablespoons vegetable oil
  or ghee
4 green cardamon pods (use
  the seeds only)

2½ cups water

---

½ cup milk

¼ teaspoon kewra essence
  (optional)

---

Decoration:
silver leaf (optional)
1 tablespoon pistachio nuts,
  unsalted or salt washed off,
  chopped
1 tablespoon raisins, soaked in
  hot water for 10 minutes (to
  soften them)

¼ cup khoa (see recipe p. 24)
  or unsweetened evaporated
  milk
2 tablespoons date sugar

1) Carefully wash and drain the rice.

2) Honey syrup: In a saucepan, bring 1/3 cup of water and honey to a boil. Add a pinch of saffron. Keep boiling and stirring until it is a sticky syrup. Then put aside to cool.

3) In a large thick-bottomed pot, heat the vegetable oil or ghee and briefly fry the green cardamon seeds and rice. Immediately add 2½ cups of water. Cover, bring to a boil again, then lower to simmer and cook until all the water is absorbed (about 20 minutes).

4) Add the milk and honey syrup (step 2). Continue cooking until the milk and syrup are absorbed and the rice is tender. Add the (optional) kewra essence and stir.

5) Place in a serving dish and (optional) decorate with silver leaf. Mix the khoa or evaporated milk with the date sugar and sprinkle that on top. On top of that sprinkle pistachios and raisins.

Yield: approximately 3 cups

# Rice and Mung Beans
## (Kicharee)

A solid staple of the traditional Indian diet — fortifying and mildly spicy. Good with plain yogurt.

| | |
|---|---|
| 1 cup whole green mung beans | 16 cups water |
| 2 cups rice | 2-3 teaspoons salt, to taste |

| | |
|---|---|
| ½ cup vegetable oil or ghee | 4 inch piece of fresh ginger, |
| 2 medium onions, chopped | peeled and chopped fine |
| 8 cloves garlic, chopped | |

| | |
|---|---|
| 1 small cinnamon stick | 1 teaspoon cumin seeds |
| 6 whole cloves | ½ teaspoon ground black |
| 4 green cardamon pods | pepper, or to taste |

1) Carefully pick over the beans and wash them. Carefully wash the rice and drain. Mix the rice and beans together with the water and salt in a large, thick-bottomed pot. Cook until the beans are soft and split open and the whole thing has the consistency of a thick soup.

2) In a thick-bottomed frying pan, heat the ghee and fry the onion, garlic and ginger until light brown. Then add the cinnamon, cloves, green cardamon, cumin and black pepper and fry for 1 minute. Add this mixture to the cooked rice and beans, stir, and cook for 2-3 minutes on a low heat. Serve with plain yogurt.

Yield: 14 cups

# Split Chickpea and Fruit Rice
## (Chanaa Daal Phal Biryaanee)

Split chickpeas:

| | |
|---|---|
| 1/2 cup split chickpeas | 1/4 teaspoon salt, or to taste |
| 2 cups water | 2 bay leaves |

| | |
|---|---|
| 2 tablespoons vegetable oil or ghee | 2 tablespoons cashew nuts |
| 2 teaspoons garam masala | 6 firm (not mushy) dates, cut in long, thin slices |

Rice:

| | |
|---|---|
| 1/2 cup rice | 1 1/2 cups water |

| | |
|---|---|
| 3 tablespoons vegetable oil or ghee | 1/4 teaspoon cinnamon powder |
| 1 medium onion, cut in rounds | 1 1/2 teaspoons cumin powder |
| 1/2 teaspoon crushed dry red chiles | 1/4 teaspoon salt, or to taste |
| 4 green cardamon pods (use only the seeds) | 1/2 cup milk |

Garnish:

| | |
|---|---|
| 2 thin slices whole wheat bread | 3-4 cashews, chopped |
| 1 tablespoon vegetable oil or ghee | 1 medium tomato, sliced thin |

*To make the split chickpeas:*

1) Thoroughly pick over and wash the beans. Soak in 2 cups of water for 1 hour. Then add 1/4 teaspoon salt and the bay leaves to the water and boil until the beans are soft. Drain off the water.

2) In a large, thick-bottomed frying pan or wok, heat 2 tablespoons of vegetable oil or ghee and add the garam masala, cashew nuts and dates. Then add cooked split peas and simmer until hot.

*To make the rice:*

1) Thoroughly wash the rice and drain. In a bowl, soak the rice in 1 1/2 cups of water for 15 minutes. Then drain, but save the water for cooking.

2) In a large, thick-bottomed frying pan or wok, heat 3 tablespoons of vegetable oil or ghee and saute the onion until brown. Then add the red chile, green cardamon, cinnamon, cumin, salt and water from the rice. Bring to a boil. Add the rice and milk and cook until all the liquid evaporates and the rice is tender. Remove from the heat.

*To serve:*
1) Cut the bread into cubes and fry in 1 tablespoon of vegetable oil or ghee until brown.

2) Place the rice in a serving dish. Pour the split pea mixture over it. Then sprinkle with the bread cubes, a few chopped cashews and the sliced tomatoes.

Yield: about 3 cups

# Coconut Rice

*2 cups rice*

---

| *2 cups grated fresh coconut* | *4 cups water* |
| --- | --- |

---

| *2 tablespoons vegetable oil or* | *4 whole cloves* |
| --- | --- |
| *ghee* | *4 green cardamon pods (use* |
| *4 medium onions, chopped* | *only the seeds)* |
| *1 small cinnamon stick* | *1 teaspoon salt, or to taste* |

1) Wash the rice thoroughly, drain and set aside.

2) In an electric blender, blend 2 cups of grated fresh coconut with 4 cups of water until smooth. Set aside.

3) In a large, thick-bottomed saucepan, heat the vegetable oil or ghee and fry the onions until golden brown. Add the cinnamon, cloves, green cardamon and salt. Fry for 1 more minute. Then add the coconut-water mixture and rice. Cover and bring to a boil, then lower the heat and simmer until the rice is tender and the liquid absorbed. Turn off the heat but keep the rice covered for another 5 minutes before serving.

Yield: 5 cups rice

# Creamy Cheese and Pea Vegetable Rice
## *(Paneer Matar Pilaao)*

Children as well as adults love this dish!

*2 cups rice*

| | |
|---|---|
| *2 tablespoons vegetable oil or ghee* | *½ cup panir, cubed (see recipe p. 24)* |

| | |
|---|---|
| *1 onion, sliced in thin crescents*<br>*2 bay leaves* | *4 green cardamon pods (use only the seeds)* |

| | |
|---|---|
| *½ teaspoon red chile powder*<br>*2 teaspoons white cumin powder*<br>*¼ teaspoon cinnamon powder* | *3 whole cloves*<br>*1 cup green peas, fresh or frozen*<br>*3 cups water* |

*1 teaspoon salt*

1) Carefully wash and drain the rice.

2) In a large, thick-bottomed frying pan, heat oil or ghee and fry the panir cubes to a light brown. Remove from the oil and set aside.

3) In the same oil, fry the onions, bay leaves and green cardamon seeds until the onions are golden brown. Add the red chile, white cumin, cinnamon and cloves, peas, fried panir and water. Bring these ingredients to a boil.

4) Add the rice and salt, cover and cook on a low heat until the water is absorbed and each grain of rice is separate. Continue to cook on a very low heat until the rice is tender. Keep covered, remove from the heat, and let stand for 15 minutes before serving.

Yield: 7 cups

# Royal Sweet Rice
## (Shaahee Mithee Pilaao)

2 cups rice

---

½ cup vegetable oil or ghee
6 green cardamon pods (use
   only the seeds)

1½ cups water

---

¾ cup honey

½ teaspoon kewra essence
   (optional)

---

2 tablespoons almonds,
   soaked and peeled
2 tablespoons pistachios,
   unsalted or salt washed off
½ cup khoa (see recipe p. 24)
   or unsweetened,
   evaporated milk

silver leaf (for decoration;
   optional)

1) Wash the rice carefully, drain, and then soak in enough water to cover rice for 15 minutes. Rinse again and drain.

2) In a large, thick-bottomed saucepan, heat the vegetable oil or ghee and briefly fry the cardamon seeds and rice. Add 1½ cups of water, bring to a boil, then cover and cook on a low heat until the rice is tender and all the water is absorbed.

3) Stir in the honey and (optional) kewra essence and cook on a very low heat until all the liquid is absorbed. Then mix in the almonds, pistachios and khoa or evaporated milk. Decorate with silver leaf (optional). Cover and let sit for 5-10 minutes before serving.

Yield: about 6 cups

*Story:*

# The Emperor Comes to Dinner

The Mughal Emperor Akhbar was well known as a patron of artists, musicians and holy men. When he heard of the spiritual greatness of Guru Amar Das, he decided at once to pay him a visit. Amar Das had decreed that anyone wishing to see him must first sit and eat at the Guru's langar, where rich and poor sat side by side and were served equally.

When word reached the Guru's court that the Emperor was on his way, there was great speculation as to whether he too would be expected to obey the Guru's order. After all, to offend a king carried no small penalty in those days. Nonetheless, Guru Amar Das was unwavering. Even Akhbar the Great would partake of the Guru's kitchen!

When Akhbar finally arrived, he proved that his wisdom was worthy of his reputation. He instructed his courtiers and retainers to join him as he sat in line upon the stone floor and was served a simple meal of vegetables and yogurt, dahl cooked in ghee, and steaming hot chapatis. He shared his dinner that night with Sikhs, Muslims and Hindus of all castes and classes.

So pleased was the Emperor by the tastiness of the simple feast — flavored with love and selfless service — and by the living example of brotherhood and equality, that he offered the Guru a large tract of land as a token of his esteem.

"But, Sir," the Guru replied, "to accept such a gift from a king would not be right. People might think that I am beholden to you, whereas I pledge my allegiance to the One God alone."

"In that case," Akhbar replied, "the land shall be granted to your lovely daughter, for she is the image of gracefulness and service. Now that is an offer you cannot refuse!"

Years later, the land which was granted by Akhbar became a shrine and a site of spiritual healing. A pond was excavated and, in its center, a temple of marble and gold was erected. Today, at the Golden Temple in the city of Amritsar, over ten thousand people are fed each day in the Guru's langar.

136

# Bean Dishes

Bean dishes (dahl) provide India with much of its protein. Like rice, the varieties of beans, lentils and dried peas is endless, and their uses endlessly creative — from soups to flours to main dishes to sweets. For most of the recipes given in this chapter, you can experiment and try substituting different kinds of beans and see what you come up with.

In bean cookery, the important thing is to make sure the beans are very well cleaned and very well cooked. Pick out all the little stones and pebbles and wash thoroughly. Thorough cooking helps reduce intestinal gas, as does fresh ginger which is included in most dahl recipes. In addition, chewing on a green cardamon pod after a meal or having a cup of mint tea helps avoid gas.

There is a shortcut to the overnight soaking which many beans require. Just boil the beans in salted water for 10 minutes. Then immerse them in cold water for one hour. From that point most beans are ready to start the regular cooking procedure called for in the recipe.

Another shortcut is to cook the beans in a pressure cooker. The cooking time will be shorter and the beans themselves creamier and even more delicious.

Bean dishes complement dry (not soupy) vegetable dishes. Such bean dishes as chickpeas and kidney beans are easy to prepare and good to serve for large gatherings.

When serving beans, you may wish to include one bowl of finely chopped jalapeno peppers and/or one bowl of finely chopped onions as a do-it-yourself garnish on your table. That way each person can add zest to his or her beans as taste dictates. This is especially useful for such bland bean dishes as mung beans.

# Cholay
## (Chole)

Garbanzo beans and potatoes are a winning combination. This very filling, flavorful dish is a north Indian standard.

For the beans:

2 cups chickpeas (garbanzo beans)

3 whole cloves

2 green cardamon pods (use only the seeds)

1½ teaspoons baking soda

2 teaspoons salt

10 cups water

---

For the sauce:

2 medium potatoes, boiled, peeled and cut in medium-sized pieces

½ cup fresh ginger, peeled and sliced in long thin slices

1 onion, sliced

4 teaspoons ground black pepper

4 teaspoons mango powder

4 teaspoons cumin powder

4 teaspoons garam masala

1 teaspoon salt, or to taste

---

Garnish:

6 teaspoons fresh coriander leaves, chopped

2 green chiles, mild or hot, to taste, chopped fine

½ cup hot ghee

2 tomatoes, sliced

4 lemons, washed and sliced thin

*To make the chickpeas (garbanzo beans):*
1) Carefully pick over and wash the beans and drain. In a large pot, *soak them overnight* in 10 cups of water, along with the cloves, green cardamon seeds and baking soda.

2) Then cook on a low heat in the same water, with salt added, until the chickpeas are tender. Drain off and discard the liquid and set the chickpeas aside.

*To make the sauce:*
1) In a large, thick-bottomed frying pan or wok, mix together the potatoes, cooked chickpeas, ginger, onion, black pepper, mango powder, cumin, garam masala and salt. Cook on a low heat, stirring well so that the spices are thoroughly mixed in.

2) Remove from the heat. Place in a serving bowl.

*Garnish:*
Sprinkle coriander leaves and green chiles on top. Then make a hollow in the center and pour in the hot ghee. Decorate with tomato and lemon slices.

Yield: 7-8 cups

# Mung Bean Dahl
## *(Moong Kee Daal)*

| | |
|---|---|
| *½ pound green mung beans (whole)* | *6 cups water* |

| | |
|---|---|
| *½ teaspoon salt, or to taste* | *1 medium onion, chopped* |
| *1 teaspoon turmeric* | *1 inch piece fresh ginger,* |
| *1 teaspoon red chile powder* | *peeled and finely chopped* |
| *4 tablespoons vegetable oil or ghee* | *1 teaspoon garam masala* |

Optional garnish:
| | |
|---|---|
| *½ cup jalapeno peppers, finely chopped* | *½ cup onions, finely chopped* |

1) Carefully pick over and wash the beans. Bring the water to a boil and add the beans and salt. Cover and cook over a medium heat. When the beans start to split open, add the turmeric and red chile and cook until it has a thick, soupy consistency. Stir frequently to prevent sticking. *Or,* pressure cook for ½ hour with 5 cups water, adding turmeric and red chile (after releasing the pressure) half way through.

2) In a thick-bottomed frying pan, heat the vegetable oil or ghee and saute the onion and ginger until golden brown. Stir in the garam masala and add this mixture to the cooked beans.

3) If you like, garnish with chopped jalapenos and onions.

Yield: 5 cups

# Channa
## (Chanaa)

Spicy chickpeas in ghee.

For the beans:

1 pound (2⅓ cups) chickpeas
(garbanzo beans)
8 cups water

1 teaspoon baking soda
½ teaspoon salt

For the sauce:

1 tablespoon pomegranate
powder or lemon juice
1 tablespoon garam masala
4 teaspoons ground black
pepper (optional: 2
teaspoons ground black
pepper and 2 teaspoons
crushed red chiles)

4 teaspoons salt
2 teaspoons turmeric
2 teaspoons fresh ginger,
peeled and chopped
2 medium potatoes, boiled,
peeled and diced

Garnish:

½ cup hot ghee
a few, fresh coriander leaves
3-6 green chiles, mild or hot,
to taste, chopped fine

1 large tomato, chopped
4 lemons, washed and sliced

*To make the beans:*
1) Carefully pick over and wash the chickpeas. *Soak them overnight* in 8 cups of water with the baking soda dissolved in it. Cook the beans in this water, adding ½ teaspoon salt, on a low heat until tender.

2) Strain off the water, setting it aside to use in the sauce.

*To make the sauce:*
1) In a large bowl, mix together the pomegranate powder (or lemon juice), garam masala, black pepper, salt, turmeric, fresh ginger and potatoes.

2) In a large, thick-bottomed saucepan or wok, combine this mixture with the cooked chickpeas. Make a hollow in the center

and pour in the water from the cooked chickpeas. Cook on a low heat until only ½ cup of water is left.

3) Heat the ghee to smoking point and pour into the middle of the chickpea mixture. Sprinkle with coriander leaves, green chiles, tomato and lemon slices.

Yield: 7 cups

# Black Bean Dahl
## (Makee Daal Dulee)

| | |
|---|---|
| 1 cup whole black beans | 1½-2 teaspoons salt |
| 6 cups water | 1 teaspoon turmeric |

| | |
|---|---|
| ½ cup vegetable oil or ghee | 1 tablespoon fresh ginger, |
| 1 medium onion, chopped | peeled and finely chopped |

| | |
|---|---|
| 1½ teaspoons cumin powder | 1 teaspoon ground black |
| 2 green chiles, mild or hot, to | pepper |
| taste, chopped | 1 medium tomato, chopped |
| 2 teaspoons fresh coriander | |
| leaves, chopped | |

1) Carefully pick over and wash the beans. Soak in 6 cups of water for 10 minutes. Then add the salt and turmeric and boil until the beans are soft, yet each bean still remains separate. Remove from the heat. Or, beans can be pressure cooked in 5 cups water for ½ hour.

2) In a large, thick-bottomed frying pan or wok, heat the vegetable oil or ghee and saute the onions and ginger until light brown. Then add the cooked beans, cumin, chiles, coriander leaves, black pepper and tomato. Stir and cook for 2 more minutes.

Yield: 5 cups

# Black Beans with Cream
## (Makhnee Urad Daal

Serve this mild, but still somewhat spicy (hot) dish with a flavorful dish such as Pumpkin Bartha.

1 pound (about 2½ cups) split black mung beans (urad dahl)

1 tablespoon fresh ginger, peeled and chopped

1 teaspoon chopped garlic

6 green chiles, mild or hot, to taste, chopped fine

½ teaspoon baking soda

2-3 teaspoons salt, or to taste

---

½ cup vegetable oil or ghee

4 medium onions, chopped

---

4 medium tomatoes, chopped

½ cup yogurt

½ cup fresh cream

1 teaspoon dry, crushed red chiles

---

Garnish:

1 tablespoon chopped, fresh coriander leaves

2 tablespoons raisins

2 tablespoons almonds. chopped

1) Carefully pick over and wash the beans. In a large, thick-bottomed pot, cook the beans, ginger, garlic, green chiles, baking soda and salt in 2½ quarts of water on a low heat until the beans are soft (approximately 1 hour).

2) In a thick-bottomed frying pan, heat the ghee or vegetable oil and fry the onions until light brown. Then add the tomatoes, yogurt, cream and crushed red chiles and cook until the oil starts to separate out. Cook 5 minutes more, stirring frequently.

3) Add the spice mixture to the cooked beans and cook for 5 minutes more. If more water is needed, add 1 cup of hot water. Continue cooking, stirring often to prevent sticking, until it becomes thick.

4) Garnish with coriander leaves, raisins and chopped almonds.

Yield: 12-14 cups

# Kidney Bean Dahl
## *(Raaj Maah)*

Very good with plain rice and raita.

| | |
|---|---|
| 1/2 pound (about 1 1/3 cups) red kidney beans | 5 cups water |

| | |
|---|---|
| 4 onions<br>1 inch piece of fresh ginger, peeled and chopped | 6 cloves garlic, sliced |

| | |
|---|---|
| 4 tablespoons vegetable oil or ghee<br>1 tablespoon water<br>1 teaspoon crushed, dry red chiles | 1 1/2 teaspoons salt, or to taste<br>1 tomato, sliced |

Garnish:

| | |
|---|---|
| 1 teaspoon garam masala | a few fresh coriander leaves, chopped |

1) Carefully pick over and wash the beans. *Soak overnight* in water. Drain.

2) In an electric blender, blend together the onions, ginger and garlic until they form a paste.

3) In a large, thick-bottomed frying pan or wok, heat the vegetable oil or ghee and fry the paste until it is golden brown, stirring continuously to prevent sticking. Then stir in 1 tablespoon of water and add the red chile, salt and tomato. Cook until the oil starts to separate out.

4) Add the beans and mix well. Add 6 cups of water and cook on a medium heat until the beans are mushy. (Otherwise they will be indigestible.) Or, pressure cook for 25-30 minutes using 5 1/2 cups water.

5) To serve, sprinkle with garam masala and coriander leaves.

Yield: 5-6 cups

# Saucy Chickpeas
## *(Khataa Chanaa)*

For the beans:

| | |
|---|---|
| 1 pound (about 2⅓ cups) chickpeas (garbanzo beans) | 1 teaspoon baking soda |
| 10 cups water | 1 black tea bag |
| | 2 teaspoons salt |

For the sauce:

| | |
|---|---|
| 2 medium potatoes, boiled, peeled and diced | 4 teaspoons turmeric |
| ½ cup fresh ginger, peeled and thinly sliced | 8 black peppercorns |
| 8 green chiles, mild or hot, to taste, chopped fine | 4 teaspoons cumin powder |
| 2 tablespoons pomegranate seeds | 3 tablespoons garam masala |
| | 2 teaspoons salt |
| | 1 cup hot ghee |

Garnish:

| | |
|---|---|
| a few, fresh coriander leaves | 2 onions, sliced thin |
| 1 cup tomatoes, chopped | 4 lemons, sliced |

*To make the beans:*

1) Carefully pick over and wash the beans. *Soak them overnight* in 5 cups of water, along with the baking soda and black tea bag.

2) In the same water, cook the beans, along with ½ teaspoon salt, on a low heat until tender. Then strain off the liquid, saving it for the gravy.

*To make the sauce:*

In a large, thick-bottomed frying pan or wok, mix together the cooked beans, potatoes, ginger (saute ginger first, if you prefer), green chiles, pomegranate seeds, turmeric, peppercorns, cumin, garam masala and salt. Make a hollow in the center and into it pour approximately 2 cups of the water from the cooked beans. Bring it to a boil and mix in the spices and the beans. Pour very hot ghee on top of it and let it simmer for 2 minutes.

*To serve:*

Place in a serving dish and garnish with coriander leaves, tomatoes, onions and lemon slices.

Yield: 11 cups

# Relishes and Pickles

Relishes (chutneys) and pickles *(achaar)* are the exclamation points of Indian food. They are perky little extras that bring a sparkle to the palate. At nearly every Indian meal or snack, there are one or two chutneys to add taste and variety.

Some relishes can be prepared in advance and stored, while others should be served soon after they are made. Chutneys made with herbs, like Mint Chutney, keep for a few days in the refrigerator. Vegetable chutneys, like Carrot Chutney, should be prepared just before serving. Pickles and fruit chutneys can be kept in jars in the refrigerator for a long time.

# Carrot Chutney
## (Gaajar Kee Chatnee)

A tangy, sweet-and-sour side dish.

1 cup grated carrots
1 cup water
2 cloves garlic, chopped fine

2 tablespoons fresh ginger,
  peeled and chopped

---

1 cup cider vinegar
3/4 cup honey
1/2 teaspoon green cardamon
  seeds
1/2 teaspoon red chile powder

2 teaspoons salt
1 tablespoon cornstarch
1/4 cup cashew nuts or 8
  soaked, peeled almonds

---

2 teaspoons raisins (which
  have been soaked in water
  for 10 minutes, then
  drained)

1) Wash, peel and grate the carrots into a saucepan. Add the water, garlic and ginger and cook until the carrots are tender and all the water has evaporated.

2) Add the vinegar, honey, cardamon seeds, red chile, salt, cornstarch and nuts and cook until the mixture is golden brown and slightly thick. Then add the raisins and cook for a few minutes.

3) Let cool and store in a covered jar in the refrigerator.

Yield: about 2½ cups

# Yogurt Chutney
## (Dahee Chatnee)

Spicy and fresh tasting — very refreshing!

1/2 cup fresh mint leaves
3 green chiles, mild or hot, to
  taste

3 teaspoons mango powder
1/4 teaspoon salt, or to taste
1/2 cup yogurt

1) In an electric blender, blend together the mint leaves, green chiles, mango powder and salt (add a little water if necessary to get it to blend).

2) In a bowl, beat the yogurt with a whisk or an eggbeater so it is creamy. Add the blended ingredients and stir well.

Yield: ¾-1 cup

# Tomato Chutney
## (Tamaatar Chatnee)

The Indian version of America's favorite chutney — ketchup!

| | |
|---|---|
| 1 pound tomatoes | 3 cloves garlic, chopped |
| 2 teaspoons chopped onions | 1 teaspoon red chile powder, |
| 3 tablespoons fresh ginger, | mild or hot, to taste |
| peeled and sliced very thin | 1 teaspoon salt |

| | |
|---|---|
| ½ cup apple cider vinegar | 12 almonds, soaked, peeled |
| ½ cup honey | and slivered |
| ¼ teaspoon black cardamon | 8 green cardamon pods (use |
| powder | only the seeds) |
| 3 tablespoons raisins | |

1) Peel the tomatoes by dipping them in boiling water. The skins will shrivel up and be easy to peel off. Then cut the tomatoes into small pieces.

2) In a thick-bottomed saucepan, mix together the tomatoes, onions, ginger, garlic, chile powder and salt and cook until the tomatoes are mushy and the sauce is thick.

3) Add the vinegar, honey, black cardamon, green cardamon seeds, raisins and almonds. (Note: To peel the almonds, place them in a bowl and cover them with boiling water for a few minutes. Remove from the water. You should be able to just "pinch" the skins right off.) Continue to cook until the mixture gets quite thick. Remove from the heat and let cool. Store in jars in the refrigerator. It will keep for a month.

Yield: about 2 cups

147

# Sweet Chutney
## (Sonth)

Easy to prepare, and very tasty.

3/4 cup water
1/2 cup mango powder
1 teaspoon red chile powder
2 teaspoons salt
1 teaspoon garam masala
1 teaspoon ginger powder

1 teaspoon white cumin
    powder
1/4 teaspoon black salt (use
    regular salt if not available)
1/2 cup honey

Boil the water and add the mango powder, chile powder, regular salt, garam masala, ginger, cumin and black salt. Remove from the heat. Stir in the honey and let cool.

Note: The black salt will smell like sulfur while cooking, but the smell disappears after the chutney cools.

Yield: approximately 2 cups

# Sweet Fruit Chutney

A fancy version of "sweet chutney" — delicious!

2 cups water
1/2 cup mango powder
1/2 teaspoon black salt (use
    regular salt if not available)

2 1/2 teaspoons red chile
    powder
1/2 cup fresh ginger, peeled
    and chopped

1/2 teaspoon white cumin
    seeds
1/2 teaspoon garam masala

1/2 teaspoon salt, or to taste
1/2 cup raisins

1/2 cup honey
4 bananas, peeled and sliced
    thin

1/2 teaspoon beet juice (for
    coloring; optional)

148

Boil the water. Add the mango powder, black salt, chile powder, ginger, cumin, garam masala, regular salt and raisins. Remove from the heat. Stir in the honey and bananas and the beet juice. Let sit for 1 hour before serving.

Note: The black salt makes a strong sulfur smell while cooking, but the smell disappears after the dish cools.

Yield: about 5 cups

# Mango Chutney
## (Amb Chatnee)

A sweet, spicy chutney for pakoras, samosas, etc.

2 green mangoes (unripe)
1/2 cup water
2 tablespoons fresh ginger,
  peeled and sliced very thin

1 tablespoon raisins
2 cloves garlic

---

1/4 cup vinegar
3 tablespoons chopped
  almonds
1/4 teaspoon black cardamon
  powder

1/4 teaspoon red chile powder
3/4 cup honey
2 teaspoons salt

1) Peel the mangoes and cut the pulp into small pieces. Place in a saucepan and cook with the water, ginger, raisins and garlic. When the mango is tender, remove from the heat.

2) Add the vinegar, almonds, cardamon, chile powder, honey and salt and mix well. Cook until the mixture is thick and brown.

3) Let cool and store in a jar in the refrigerator.

Yield: 3 cups

# Spicy Sweet and Sour Mango Chutney
## (Naavratan Chatnee)

Sweet and mildly salty. Great with chapatis!

2 unripe mangoes (about 3
  cups)
1/2 cup water

4 bay leaves
5 teaspoons salt

---

1/2 cup dried dates (without
  pits)

1/2 cup vinegar

---

1/2-3/4 cup honey
1/2 cup vinegar
1/2 teaspoon ground black
  pepper
1 teaspoon crushed dry red
  chiles
1 teaspoon ginger powder

1 teaspoon black cumin seeds
  (if not available, use white)
1 teaspoon cinnamon powder
1/2 teaspoon clove powder
1/2 teaspoon nutmeg powder
1/2 teaspoon cardamon
  powder

---

1/2 cup almonds, roasted and
  slivered
1/2 cup raisins

2 tablespoons pistachio nuts
  (shelled)
1 tablespoon fresh lime juice

1) Peel the mangoes and grate finely or chop into small pieces. Place in a thick-bottomed saucepan and add the water, bay leaves and salt. Cover and simmer on a low heat until the mango starts getting soft. Be sure to stir now and then to prevent sticking.

2) Clean the dates and simmer in 1/2 cup vinegar until soft. Then strain off the vinegar, let the dates cool and slice them very thin.

3) In a thick-bottomed saucepan mix together the honey and another 1/2 cup of vinegar, add the mangoes (step 1), dates (step 2), black pepper, crushed chiles, ginger powder, cumin, cinnamon, clove, nutmeg and cardamon. Cook until it becomes a thick puree, stirring frequently. Then add the almonds, raisins, pistachios and lime juice, and continuing to stir, simmer gently until it becomes thick. Let cool and store in a jar in the refrigerator.

Yield: approximately 4 cups

# Mint Chutney
## (Poodeenaa Imlee Chatnee)

Five-minute chutney — spicy, hot and very tasty. Very good with chapatis and bland dishes. A little goes a long way!

½ cup fresh mint leaves, chopped
2 tablespoons seedless tamarind concentrate (dissolved in 2 tablespoons of hot water), dry pomegranate seeds or lemon juice

2 tablespoons honey
2 green chiles, mild or hot, to taste
pinch of salt

In an electric blender, blend all the ingredients. Serve fresh.

Yield: ⅔ cup


# Mint and Coriander Chutney
## (Poodeenaa Dhaneeaa Kee Chatnee)

A delicious, spicy chutney for samosas or pakoras.

4 tablespoons fresh coriander leaves
4 tablespoons fresh mint leaves
2 green chiles, mild or hot, to taste

2 teaspoons salt
2 tablespoons seedless tamarind concentrate
2 tablespoons honey
8 tablespoons water

In an electric blender, blend all the ingredients. Serve fresh.

Yield: 1 cup

# Lemon Chutney
## (Nimboo Chatnee)

No cooking — a pungent, sweet, sour and salty chutney.

*4 lemons*

---

*1 tablespoon salt*
*¼ teaspoon red chile powder*
*3 whole cloves, ground*

*1 black cardamon pod (use*
  *only the seeds)*
*⅓ cup honey*

1) Carefully wash, dry and juice the lemons. Then remove the pulp and discard it. Chop the peels very fine and add them to the lemon juice. Cover and let sit, unrefrigerated, *for 3 or 4 days.*

2) Then add the salt, red chile, cloves, cardamon seeds and honey. Store in a jar in the refrigerator. It will keep for several weeks.

Yield: 1½ cups


# Turnip, Carrot and Cauliflower Pickle
## (Shalgam, Gaajar, Gobee Achaar)

A substantial, somewhat spicy side dish that complements simple rice dishes and breads.

*7 cups vegetables (a combina-*
  *tion of turnips, carrots and*
  *cauliflower, chopped as*
  *indicated)*
*⅓ cup vegetable oil*

*4 teaspoons garlic cloves,*
  *peeled and crushed*
*4 teaspoons fresh ginger,*
  *peeled and crushed*
*½ cup water*

---

*½ cup fructose*
*¼ cup cider vinegar*
*1 teaspoon crushed dry red*
  *chiles*

*8 teaspoons garam masala*
*1 teaspoon mustard powder*
*1 teaspoon salt*

1) Wash the vegetables thoroughly. Cut the carrots (peeled) and cauliflower into medium-sized pieces. Do not peel the turnips but cut them into medium-sized pieces.

2) Heat a large pot of water to boiling, add the vegetables and leave them until the water begins to boil again. Then strain off the water and spread the vegetables out on paper towels or a clean cloth.*Let them sit for 2 hours.* Then gather them into a bowl and let them sit, unrefrigerated and uncovered, *overnight.*

3) In a thick-bottomed frying pan, heat the oil to smoking point. Remove the pan from the heat and let the oil cool. Then add the garlic and ginger, return to the heat and fry until they are brown. Add ½ cup of water and cook until all the water is evaporated.

4) Soak the fructose in the vinegar. Stir in the crushed chiles, garam masala, mustard powder, salt and garlic/ginger mix (step 1). Add all the vegetables and mix well. Then pack in a large jar (or jars) and place in the sun. Be sure to stir it well at least once a day. *Fifteen days after bottling,* the pickles are ready to eat. Then store in jars and refrigerate.

Yield: approximately 6 cups

# Stuffed Red Pepper Pickle
## (Mirchee Kaa Achaar)

A strong-bodied, spicy, moderately hot condiment.

| | |
|---|---|
| 1 cup fresh red chiles, large size (or small yellow chiles) | 1 cup mustard oil |

| | |
|---|---|
| 4 teaspoons fenugreek powder | 7-8 teaspoons salt |
| 9 teaspoons garam masala | 3 teaspoons mango powder |
| 2-3 teaspoons red chile powder | 2 teaspoons white cumin powder |
| 8 teaspoons fennel seed powder | 1 teaspoon mace powder |

juice of 1 or 2 lemons

1) Wash and dry the fresh red chiles. Cut lengthwise, scrape out the seeds and cut off the stem.

2) Heat the oil until very hot. Then remove the pan from the heat and let cool.

3) In a bowl, mix together all the spices. Pour ½ cup of cooled oil over the spices and mix well. Then stuff this mixture into the fresh red chiles.

4) Put the chiles in a jar, then pour in the rest of the oil and the lemon juice. *Let sit, unrefrigerated, for 15 days.* Stir it occasionally. Then store in a jar in the refrigerator.

Yield: 1½ cups

# Beverages

India's beverages tend to be fairly simple: a fruit punch, warm sweetened milk or tea. They are either served alone or with snacks. Meals are accompanied by cool, pure water.

Lassi, a blended yogurt drink, is a wonderful, mid-afternoon pick-me-up. Lassi comes in three varieties: with a little salt, a little honey, or just plain, depending on your taste and mood that day.

The warm milk drinks are good sources of protein and energy. Their warmth and high-calcium content make them particularly soothing pre-bedtime drinks.

Jaljeera is a spicy beverage that acts as an appetite stimulant when served chilled before a meal, or, served warm, accompanies golgappas, the little pillow-like snack wafers, as both a filling and a dip.

# Date Milk
## (Khajool Dudh)

This drink is especially good in the evening.

| | |
|---|---|
| 4 firm dates (not mushy), without pits | 1/2 cup water |
| 2 cups milk | 5 almonds, sliced |

In a thick-bottomed saucepan, boil the dates in the water for about 2 minutes. When the dates are soft, mash them with a fork and add the milk and almonds. Bring to a boil, then simmer for 2 more minutes and remove from the heat. Serve with dates still in (blending optional).

Yield: approximately 2 cups

# Milk with Ghee and Almonds
## (Badaam Dudh)

A great bedtime snack!

| | |
|---|---|
| 1 tablespoon ghee | 6 almonds, sliced or slivered |
| 2 cardamon pods (use the seeds only) | 2 cups milk |
| 1-2 teaspoons honey (to taste) | |

In a thick-bottomed frying pan, heat the ghee and saute the almonds until they start getting brown. Crush the cardamon seeds and add along with the milk. Boil for 1 minute. Add honey to taste.
Serve with almonds and cardamon seeds still in (blending optional).

Yield: about 2 cups

# Jaljeera
## (Jaljeeraa)

A spicy sip or dip. Good as an appetizer or with golgappas, this "Indian lemonade" has an exotic, spicy, salty-sweet flavor.

2 quarts water
3/8 cup tamarind concentrate
  (seedless)
2 small bunches of fresh mint
  leaves
1/2 teaspoon garam masala
2 teaspoons black salt or sea
  salt, if black salt is not
  available

1/8 cup fresh ginger, peeled
  and chopped
2 tablespoons honey
6 green chiles, mild or hot, to
  taste
2 tablespoons white cumin
  powder
the juice of 1/2 lemon

1) In an electric blender, blend 1½ cups of the water (reserving the rest of the water) with all the other ingredients. When totally blended, stir into the remaining water.

2) Serve cool as a beverage, or hot as a dip with golgappas (see recipe p. 49). Golgappas are extremely thin, hollow wafers. To eat them you can make a small hole in the side, fill the golgappa with jaljeera and then very, very quickly pop the whole thing into your mouth. Speed is of the essence, otherwise you end up with a handful of wet crumbs and a lapful of jaljeera. First timers can try just dipping the golgappas in the jaljeera; the taste, in the end, is the same.

Yield: about 8½ cups

# Seera with Whole Wheat Flour

Dessert in a tea cup! Good as a snack or before bed; also good for colds and flu.

| | |
|---|---|
| 1 tablespoon whole wheat flour | 1 tablespoon ghee |

| | |
|---|---|
| 5 almonds, soaked, peeled and shredded | 2 cardamon pods (seeds only) |
| 5 pistachios, unsalted or salt washed off, shredded | 5 raisins |

| | |
|---|---|
| 10 ounces of water | 1 tablespoon honey, or to taste |

1) Saute flour in ghee on a low heat till light brown. Add almonds, pistachios, cardamon seeds and raisins. Stir well.

2) Add water, let cook till the consistency is like thick soup, then add honey and serve hot.

Yield: 8 ounces

# Seera with Chickpea Flour

A hearty, spicy drink, good for sore throats and congested noses and chests.

| | |
|---|---|
| 10 almonds, soaked and peeled | 4 cardamon pods (seeds only) |
| 10 pistachios, unsalted or salt washed off | ¼ cup water |

| | |
|---|---|
| 1 tablespoon chickpea flour | 2 tablespoons ghee |

| | |
|---|---|
| 8 ounces of milk | 1 tablespoon of honey, or to taste |

1) Blend almonds, pistachios and cardamon seeds together in the water, making a paste.

2) Saute the flour in the ghee on a low heat until light brown. Add the paste from step 1. Stir well.

3) Add milk and honey and cook for a few minutes on medium heat, stirring constantly so that the milk will not curdle. Ready to serve.

Yield: 10 ounces

# Energy Drink
## (Shardaee)

A sweet, spicy, milky drink — very refreshing in the summer.

50 almonds (about ¼ cup)
1 tablespoon cantaloupe seeds
1 tablespoon watermelon
  seeds
1 tablespoon sunflower seeds
1 tablespoon pumpkin seeds

3 tablespoons poppy
  (khaskhas) seeds
5 cardamon pods (green, if
  possible; seeds only)
10 black peppercorns
1 cup water

8-10 tablespoons honey, to
  taste

5 cups water
4 ice cubes (optional)

Thoroughly blend all the nuts, seeds, and spices in 1 cup water until a thick paste is formed. Add honey, 5 cups water and (optional) ice cubes, blend and serve. Or, let sit in the refrigerator until cold.

Yield: 6½ cups, enough for 8 people

# Saffron Milk
## (Kesree Dudh)

A warm, fragrant, curl-up-with-a-book morning or before-bed drink.

| | |
|---|---|
| *5 threads of saffron* | *2 tablespoons water* |

| | |
|---|---|
| *1 cup milk* | *5 almonds, chopped* |
| *4 green cardamon pods (use only the crushed seeds)* | *1 teaspoon honey, or to taste* |

1) Soak the saffron in 2 tablespoons of water for 5 minutes.

2) Boil the milk with the green cardamon seeds for 1 minute. Then add the saffron water and almonds. Remove from the heat. Add honey to taste and stir. Serve with almonds and cardamon seeds still in (blending optional).

Yield: about 1 cup

# Saffron Milk with Almonds
## (Kesar Dadaam Dudh)

A filling, flavorful drink. Serve hot for colds and chest congestion, or cold for an energy lift.

| | |
|---|---|
| *10 ounces of milk* | *6 threads of saffron* |
| *4 cardamon pods (seeds only)* | |

| | |
|---|---|
| *5 pistachios, unsalted or washed off* | *1 tablespoon honey, or to taste* |
| *5 almonds, soaked and peeled* | *2 ice cubes (optional)* |

1) Cook milk on medium heat with cardamon seeds and saffron threads until 8 ounces of milk remain.

2) Blend with nuts and honey and serve hot, or add ice cubes for cold "smoothie."

Yield: 8 ounces

# Golden Milk

A cozy drink before bed.

1 teaspoon ghee
1/2 teaspoon turmeric
8 ounces milk

1 tablespoon honey, or to
taste

Heat ghee. Add turmeric and stir well. Now add milk, and once more stir. Let cook for 1 minute on medium heat, then add honey and stir. Ready to serve.

Yield: about 6 ounces


# Banana-Almond Protein Drink

A quick breakfast energy drink.

8 ounces of milk
1 tablespoon of protein
    powder
1/2 ripe banana
10 almonds, soaked and
    peeled

10 pistachios, unsalted or salt
    washed off
4 cubes ice
1 tablespoon honey, or to
    taste

Blend all the ingredients together thoroughly. Ready to serve.

Yield: 2 cups

# Fruit Shake

A light, delightful shake for breakfast or as a snack

6 ounces milk
4 cubes ice
2 cardamon pods (seeds only)

1 cup any seasonal fruit
1-2 tablespoons honey, to
   taste

Blend all ingredients together thoroughly. Ready to serve.

Yield: about 14 ounces

# Mango Shake

Delicious and satisfying!

8 ounces milk
pulp of one mango
1 tablespoon honey, or to
   taste or 1 tablespoon
   sandalwood syrup or 2 drops
   sandalwood essence and 1
   tablespoon honey

2 cardamon pods (seeds only)
4 ice cubes

Blend all the ingredients together thoroughly. Ready to serve.

Note: If sandalwood syrup (or sandalwood essence and honey) is substituted for honey in this recipe, the drink, taken once a day for a month, is said to help make the brain alert, help prevent headache, and assist in chronic mucus problems.

Yield: about 18 ounces

# Mango Drink

In consistency, rather like a fruit juice, this refreshing drink is said to prevent heat stroke.

*pulp of 1 mango, diced*
*3 cups water*

*2 tablespoons honey, or to taste*

Cook the mango in the water until very soft. Then place, along with honey, in blender and thoroughly blend. Refrigerate until cold, then serve.

Yield: about 3 cups

# Plum Drink

A light, fruity drink for summer weather. Said to help prevent heat stroke and liver problems.

*5 dried plums (prunes)*

*16 ounces water*

---

*pinch of salt*
*1 tablespoon honey*

*pinch of black pepper*

---

*2 cubes ice*

1) Soak plums in water *overnight.*

2) In the morning, boil till only half the water is left.

3) Add remaining ingredients and stir well. Let cool, then serve with ice.

Yield: 10 ounces

# Indian Tea

Indians are notorious black tea drinkers, much as Americans drink coffee. After a filling meal, there's nothing like a good cup of "chaa...." Now, thanks to decaffeinated tea bags, even health conscious Americans can enjoy this delicious drink.

| | |
|---|---|
| 2 cardamon pods (seeds only) | 10 ounces of water |

| |
|---|
| 1 bag Lipton Tea (or another black tea) |

| | |
|---|---|
| 4 almonds, soaked, peeled and shredded | 2 tablespoons milk |
| 1 tablespoon honey, or to taste | |

1) Boil cardamon seeds in water until 8 ounces of water are left. Then add tea bag, cover, remove from heat and let steep for 1 minute.

2) Add almonds, honey to taste, and milk. Ready to serve.

Yield: about 8 ounces

# Ginger Tea
## (Adrak Chaa)

Strong gingery taste — will give you energy! Also good for colds, flu, sore throats, and menstrual cramps.

| | |
|---|---|
| 1 2-inch stick fresh ginger, peeled and chopped | 10 ounces water |
| 1 1-inch stick cinnamon | 1 bag Darjeeling tea |
| 2 cardamon pods (green, if possible; seeds only) | ½ cup milk |

| |
|---|
| 1 tablespoon honey, or to taste |

Boil ginger, cinnamon and cardamon in water until only 8 ounces of water remain. Add tea bag and milk, return to a boil, add honey and stir. Strain and serve.

Yield: 1½ cups

# Yogi Tea*

My husband's special recipe. Good for the blood, the colon, the nervous system and the bones, and for colds, flu and physical weakness. That is a great deal of benefit in a small, flavorful cup of tea!

*10 ounces water*
*2 slices fresh ginger root,*
  *peeled*
*3 cloves*

*4 green cardamon pods,*
  *cracked*
*4 black peppercorns*
*½ stick cinnamon*

---

*¼ teaspoon black tea (prefer-*
  *ably Jasmine)*

---

*1 tablespoon honey, or to*
  *taste*

*½ cup milk*

1) Bring the water to a boil and add the spices. Cover and continue boiling for 10-15 minutes.

2) Remove from heat, add black tea and let steep for 1-2 minutes.

3) Add honey and milk, bring to a boil, and remove from heat. Strain and serve.

Yield: 1 cup

*Pre-measured and packaged yogi tea can be purchased in many specialty food stores.*

# Masala Tea
## (Masaalaa Chaa)

Deliciously aromatic!

2 cardamon pods (seeds only)          1 inch piece of fresh ginger
1 inch stick of cinnamon              10 ounces water

---

1 bag Lipton Tea (or another          1 tablespoon honey, or to
  black tea.)                           taste
4 almonds, soaked and peeled          ½ cup milk
5 pistachios, unsalted or salt
  washed off

Boil spices in water until 8 ounces of water are left. Add tea bag, almonds, pistachios, honey and milk, bring to a boil, and remove from heat. Strain, if desired, and serve hot — or refrigerate and serve cold.

Yield: 12 ounces unstrained


# Fennel or Oregano Tea
## (Ajwan Chaa)

A strong, somewhat stimulating tea; good for the digestion and to soothe an upset stomach.

1 tablespoon fennel seeds or          10 ounces of water
  oregano seeds

---

1 cup milk
1 bag Lipton Tea (or another
  black tea)

---

1-2 tablespoons honey, or to
  taste

Boil fennel or oregano in water until only 8 ounces of water are left. Add milk and tea bag and return to a boil. Add honey, mix well, strain and serve.

Yield: 2 cups

# Hot or Cold Lemonade

Served cold, a refreshing drink for summer days. Served hot, soothes sore throats.

*2 tablespoons honey*
*7 ounces water*

*juice of one fresh lemon*
*2 cubes ice (optional)*

Combine honey with a little warm water, mixing well till honey dissolves. Then add lemon juice and remaining water, cold or hot as desired. Optional: Blend with ice cubes in blender.

Yield: 8-10 ounces

# Cold, Salted Lemonade

Refreshingly different as a summer drink. In India, it is taken to prevent heat stroke.

*6 ounces water*
*4 ice cubes*
*juice of one fresh lemon*

*a pinch or two of salt*
*a pinch or two of black pepper*

Blend everything together thoroughly, then serve.

Yield: 10 ounces

# Lassi
## *(Lasee)*

A cold yogurt shake. Good for breakfast, snack or anytime.

*2 cups yogurt*
*2 cups water*

*2 cubes ice*

---

*4 drops rose water*
*juice of ½ lemon or ¼*
*    teaspoon nutmeg*

*pinch salt (optional) or 1 table-*
*    spoon honey (optional), or*
*    to taste*

In an electric blender, blend the yogurt and water with a few ice cubes until bubbles form on top. Put in 4 drops of rose water, add lemon juice or nutmeg and either honey or salt to taste, or leave plain, and blend again. Serve very cold.

Yield: 1 quart

# A Heavenly Dessert

Baba Sheik Farid, the great fifteenth century Muslim saint, received his early spiritual instruction from his mother. When he was but a small boy, she devised a plan to encourage him to meditate.

She told her son, "Sit quietly with your eyes closed and meditate on God. If you sit really still and concentrate very deeply, God will send down an angel to give you a reward."

While her son was meditating, she slipped into his room and hid a delicious sweet under his prayer rug. When he finished his meditation and found the treat, he ran to his mother crying, "It's true. It's true. An angel did bring me a reward!"

Farid's mother kept up this same practice every day. Years passed. One day, she noticed that hours had gone by, and Farid had not returned from his meditation. Puzzled, she went to his room and found his small body sitting straight and tall, but almost lifelessly still. Farid had gone into a deep state of meditation. Frightened as any mother would be, she called to him, "Farid, Farid, are you all right?"

The boy opened his eyes. "Don't worry mother. I'm fine. You needn't bring me sweets today. Your little trick was very helpful, but I don't need it any more. Today I've tasted the real heavenly dessert!"

Farid came to be known as "Ganj-i-Shakar," the treasury of sweetness. It is said that once, during a long fast, he placed some pebbles in his mouth to assuage his hunger. The pebbles turned into candies!

Farid's birthplace has become a sacred shrine, and to this day, a free kitchen serves food to all who visit there.

170

# Sweets and Desserts

Sweet foods play a very important part in the Indian way of life. Traditionally, meals are served in only two courses: the main course, with its rich array of bread, vegetable, yogurt and rice dishes (one of which may be sweet), followed by the sweet course. Spiritually, almost every religious ceremony includes a sweet as part of the rites of devotion, either offered to God in thanks or distributed to all as a symbol of God's blessings. And, of course, whenever snacks are served, both sweet and savory delights may be included.

Sweets are made at home, but often, with no loss of face, an Indian cook will buy sweets from a professional sweet-maker ("halwai") at the sweetshop ("mithaiwala"). Unfortunately, mithaiwalas are few and far between in the West; therefore, I have included a wide variety of recipes in this chapter so, with a little extra time and effort, you can enjoy this irresistible aspect of Indian cuisine.

Sweets can be classified in two categories. "Dry" sweets are candy-like and can be eaten with the fingers. They keep well for a long time (if hidden). "Wet" sweets are slightly moist or are served in a syrup. I have also included some cake recipes that are more Western in flavor. While not strictly traditional, they are among my favorites.

*Cream Balls and Noodles in Syrup:*

# Cheese Balls in Sweet Sauce
## (Raasgulaa)

*chenna from 1 quart milk (see*          *1 tablespoon cream of wheat*
  *recipe for "Panir," p. 24)*

---

*1 cup honey*                              *1 cup water*

1) Place the chenna in a bowl, add the cream of wheat and mix together until it forms a smooth dough. Make small balls about the size of a walnut.

2) Bring the honey and water to a boil to form a syrup. Place the balls in the boiling syrup. Cook until cracks appear in the balls. Remove from the syrup and let cool before serving.

Yield: 1 dozen balls

# Cheese Disks in Pistachio Cream Sauce
## (Ras Malaai)

For the disks:
*Chenna from 1 quart milk (see*           *1 tablespoon cream of wheat*
  *recipe for "Panir," p. 24)*

---

*1 cup honey*                              *1 cup water*

---

For the cream sauce:
*1 pint "half and half" milk*             *2 drops rose water (optional)*

---

For the topping:
*1 teaspoon pistachio nuts,*              *1 teaspoon almonds, slivered*
  *chopped*

1) Prepare the chenna and honey syrup as for Rasgulla (see recipe above), but instead of forming into balls, flatten the balls into thick

disks. Cook in honey syrup until cracks appear, then remove from the syrup, pressing them gently to remove the excess syrup. Set aside.

2) In a thick-bottomed saucepan, cook the "half and half" over a medium heat, *stirring constantly*, until it thickens. Remove from the heat, stir in rose water (optional), and soak the cheese disks in this cream for 15 minutes.

3) To serve: place the cheese disks in a bowl. Pour the cream sauce over them and sprinkle with pistachios and almonds. Chill before serving.

Yield: 1 dozen disks and 1/3 cup cream

# Sweet Cream Balls
## (Khoaa Laddoo)

6 cups milk
1/2 teaspoon citric acid
1 teaspoon ghee

2 tablespoons honey
1/4 teaspoon kewra essence

20 pistachios, chopped fine
20 almonds, slivered

silver leaf for decoration

1) In a thick-bottomed saucepan, bring the milk to a boil, then reduce the heat and continue to cook, *stirring all the time*, until thickened into khoa. Then add a few drops of citric acid, repeating this several times, so the milk becomes grainy in texture but not watery. Cook for 5 more minutes. Add 1 teaspoon of ghee and keep stirring until the ghee starts to separate out. Remove from the heat.

2) Stir in the honey and let the mixture cool. Add the kewra essence and stir. Then roll the mixture into small balls, about the size of a walnut. Arrange on a platter, and sprinkle with pistachios and almonds and decorate with silver leaf.

Yield: 14 balls

# Gulab Jaman
## *(Gulaab Jaaman)*

These honey-drenched sweet balls are an Indian favorite.

For the balls:

5 teaspoons unbleached white flour

½ teaspoon baking soda

3 teaspoons melted ghee

18 teaspoons non-instant powdered milk

2-6 teaspoons yogurt, or enough to make a soft dough

2 cups vegetable oil or ghee for deep frying

---

For the syrup:

1¼ cups honey

1 cup water

pinch of salt

---

Garnish:

¼ teaspoon kewra essence, or to taste (optional)

*To make the balls:*
1) Sift together the flour and baking soda. Work the melted ghee into this mixture with your fingertips. Add the powdered milk and enough yogurt to form a very soft dough. Roll it into small balls about the size of a walnut.

2) In a thick-bottomed saucepan, heat the vegetable oil or ghee for deep frying. Gently immerse the balls in the hot oil and deep fry on a low heat until brown. Remove with a slotted spoon, letting the excess oil drip back into the pan. Set aside.

*To make the syrup:*
Cook the honey, water and salt together until the honey is completely dissolved. Let cool. Then add the deep fried balls and let them sit in the syrup until they have soaked it all up (approximately 1 hour).

*To serve:*
Arrange on a platter (optional: sprinkle with kewra essence).

Yield: 1 dozen balls

# Gulab Jaman — American Style
## (Gulaab Jaaman)

Honey-drenched sweet balls that are easy-to-make. A very sweet treat.

For the balls:

1 cup buttermilk pancake mix

2 cups non-instant milk
   powder

⅛ teaspoon baking soda

4 teaspoons vegetable oil

1 cup lukewarm milk, or
   enough to form a smooth
   dough

2 cups vegetable oil or ghee
   for deep frying

For the syrup:

1½ cups honey

1½ cups water

*To make the balls:*
1) Sift together the buttermilk pancake mix, milk powder and baking soda. Mix in 4 teaspoons of vegetable oil. Add enough milk to form a smooth dough. Oil your hands to prevent sticking and roll the dough into small balls about the size of a walnut.

2) In a thick-bottomed saucepan or wok, heat the 2 cups of vegetable oil or ghee to a low heat for deep frying. (If the oil is too hot, the balls will not cook at the center.) Immerse the balls in the hot oil and deep fry until brown. Remove from the oil with a slotted spoon, letting the excess oil drip back into the pan. Drain further on paper towels.

*To make the syrup:*
Dissolve the honey in the water by boiling for 2 minutes. Let cool. Add the deep fried balls and let them soak in the syrup for at least 5 minutes. Serve warm or chilled. (These balls will keep for several weeks in the refrigerator.)

Yield: approximately 25 balls

# Honey Bits

Very sweet and tasty.

For the pastry:

1 cup khoa (see recipe p. 24)
   or unsweetened evaporated milk
¼ cup panir (see recipe p. 24)
½ teaspoon baking soda
½ teaspoon water
3 tablespoons cream of wheat

1 cup unbleached white flour,
   or enough to form a wet
   dough
2 cups vegetable oil or ghee
   for deep frying

---

For the syrup:

2 cups honey

2 cups water

---

For decoration:
½ cup shredded coconut

*To make the pastry:*
1) Mix the khoa and panir together well. Dilute the baking soda in ½ teaspoon water and stir in. Add the cream of wheat and enough flour to form a wet dough. Roll into thick cylinders about 2 inches long and ½ inch wide.

2) In a thick-bottomed saucepan, heat the vegetable oil or ghee for deep frying. Reduce the heat, immerse the pastry in the hot oil and deep fry until light brown. Remove with a slotted spoon, letting the excess oil drip back into the pan. Drain further on paper towels.

*To make the syrup:*
Boil the water and honey together until the honey is completely dissolved. Remove from the heat.

*Then:*
Place the pastry in the hot syrup and *soak for 3 or 4 hours.* Then remove from the syrup and cut into 1-inch thick pieces. Sprinkle with shredded coconut.

Yield: 135 1-inch by ¾-inch pastries

# Sweet Cones
## (Cham Cham)

1 1/2 cups honey                    1 1/2 cups water

---

panir (very firm) from 2 quarts        4 1/4 cups water
  of milk (see recipe p. 24)           1 teaspoon rose water
1 tablespoon cornstarch
1/4 teaspoon powdered orange
  food color* (or substitute
  enough orange liquid food
  color to color the panir
  orange)

To make the syrup:
Bring the honey and water to a boil until the honey is dissolved.
Remove from the heat.

To make the sweet cones:
1) Mash the panir with your hands into a fine curd, then mix in the
cornstarch. Mold into little cone shapes. Set aside.

2) Bring the honey and water to a boil again and mix in food color.
Carefully immerse the cones in the syrup and cook them on a
gentle heat until cracks appear in the cones.

3) Strain off 1/4 cup of this syrup water and mix it with 3/4 cup of
water. Pour this mixture back into the syrup pot, but not directly
onto the cones. Cook the cones some more until the syrup
thickens a bit.

4) Repeat step 3 two more times. Then add 2 cups of water to the
syrup pot and let it sink to the bottom. Mix in 1 teaspoon of rose
water. Remove the cones. Chill them before serving.

Yield:: 2 dozen cones

*For example, Oshwal's Orange Food Colour Powder (Oshwal Enterprises Ltd., 256
Water Road, Wembley, Middx. HAD 1QQ, England), available from Indian food
stores.

# Sweet Noodles
## *(Faloodaa)*

For the noodles:
*¾ cup arrowroot flour*
*3 cups water*
*3 cups ice in 3 cups water*

*enough cold water to cover*
*the noodles*
*or substitute noodles with 1½*
*cups thin vermicelli or rice,*
*cooked according to instruc-*
*tions on package.*

---

For the syrup:
*⅛ teaspoon kewra essence*
*1 cup water*

*⅛ teaspoon kewra essence*
*(optional)*

*To make the noodles:*
In a thick-bottomed saucepan, mix the arrowroot flour into the 3 cups of water very thoroughly. Cook on a low heat, stirring continuously, until it starts to thicken and pull away from the sides of the pot. Place this mixture in a pasta machine and press it through, out into a basin of ice water (3 cups ice and 3 cups water). Remove the noodles from the water and place in a deep dish. Cover with cold water.

Note: Cooked vermicelli may be substituted for homemade noodles.

*To make the syrup:*
Mix the honey and water together and cook until it forms a sticky syrup. Let cool, then stir in kewra essence.

*To serve:*
Remove the noodles from the water. Drain well and serve with syrup poured over them.

Yield: 1½ cups

178

# Fragrant Sweet Noodles
## (Parsee daa Saaveeaan)

Very rich and delicious as a side dish.

1/2-2/3 cup vegetable oil or ghee

1/4 cup almonds, soaked and peeled

1/4 cup raisins

1 1/2 cups noodles (see recipe p. 178 or use thin vermicelli)

2 cups water

1/2 cup honey

---

1/4 teaspoon nutmeg powder

6-8 green cardamon pods (use only the seeds, crushed)

In a large, thick-bottomed frying pan, heat the vegetable oil or ghee and saute the almonds and raisins until the almonds are a deep brown. Remove from the ghee and set aside. Then add the noodles to the pan and fry them until light brown. Add the water and honey and stir gently. Cook on a medium heat until all the water is absorbed. Then, add the nutmeg, crushed cardamon seeds and the almonds and raisins. Stir well and cook on a low heat for a few minutes. Can be served hot or cold.

Yield: 1 1/2 cups

*Ice Cream and Syrup:*

# Indian Ice Cream
## (Kulfee)

2 cups milk
4 cardamon pods (green, if
   possible; use only the
   crushed seeds)

⅔ cup khoa (see recipe p. 24)
   or unsweetened,
   evaporated milk

---

5 teaspoons unbleached white
   flour

½ cup milk

---

⅓ cup honey
1 tablespoon pistachios,
   unsalted or salt washed off,
   chopped

2 tablespoons almonds,
   soaked, peeled and slivered
¼ teaspoon kewra essence

1) In a thick-bottomed saucepan, bring the 2 cups of milk, with the green cardamon pods in it, to a boil. Add the khoa or unsweetened evaporated milk and cook for 15 minutes, *stirring continuously* .

2) In a bowl, mix the flour and ½ cup of milk together to form a paste. Add this to the boiling milk, stirring it in thoroughly. Continue to cook and stir until the mixture thickens.

3) Remove from the heat and add the honey, stirring thoroughly. Mix in the pistachios, almonds and kewra essence.

4) Pour into an ice-cube tray and freeze. Serve with noodles (see recipe p. 178) or serve alone like ice cream.

Yield: 3 cups

# Mango Sherbet

A fruity treat, nice over ice cream or in making mango shakes or mango lassis.

4 ripe mangoes or 1 cup
  mango juice
1½ cups water

¾ cup honey
1½ teaspoons citric acid
  powder

1) Extract the juice from the mangoes or use one cup of mango juice.

2) In a pot, mix together the mango juice, water, honey and citric acid powder. Pour into clean bottles, cap and *let stand, unrefrigerated for 15 days* before using.

Yield: 3¼ cups

# Cheese Pudding
## *(Paneer Halwaa)*

A decorative, tasty treat.

| | |
|---|---|
| *²/₃ cup honey* | *²/₃ cup water* |

| | |
|---|---|
| *panir from I gallon of milk (see recipe p. 24)* | *3 tablespoons cornstarch* |
| *2 quarts of milk* | *¼ cup water* |
| | *½ teaspoon kewra essence* |

| | |
|---|---|
| *2 teaspoons pistachios, unsalted or salt washed off, chopped* | *3 green cardamon pods (use only the seeds)* |
| *2 teaspoons almonds, soaked, peeled and chopped* | *1 or 2 cherries, pitted and chopped* |
| *2 teaspoons cashews, chopped* | *silver leaf for decoration* |

1) In a thick-bottomed saucepan, cook the honey and water on a very low heat, being careful not to scorch, until it becomes a thick syrup (it should hang like a thread from a spoon). Grate the panir and stir it into this syrup. Continue to cook for 2 minutes. Then remove from the heat.

2) In a thick-bottomed saucepan, bring 2 quarts of milk to a boil. Mix the cornstarch with ¼ cup of water and add this to the boiling milk, stirring until it thickens slightly. Add the cooked panir, stir well and cook for 1 or 2 minutes. Then remove from the heat and mix in the kewra essence.

3) Place in a serving dish or individual dessert cups. Sprinkle with pistachios, almonds, cashews, green cardamon seeds and cherry pieces. Decorate with silver leaf. Refrigerate until serving.

Note: The consistency of this pudding is a thick liquid, not gelled as with many American puddings.

Yield: 2 quarts

# Royal Pudding
## (Shaahee Halwaa)

Very good served piping hot.

Although most Indian women do not enjoy the same freedoms and opportunities as women in the West, womanhood is very deeply respected within the Indian culture. In many villages, there is a ceremony once a year to honor the little girls — from infants up to 12-year-olds — and to pray that they may have virtuous and prosperous lives. The adults of the community give them money and wash their feet, and everyone has a big plate of Royal Pudding!

| | |
|---|---|
| 2 cups milk | 2 tablespoons honey |

| | |
|---|---|
| ⅔ cup ghee | 5 green cardamon pods (use |
| ½ cup cream of wheat | only the seeds) |
| 2 tablespoons unbleached white flour | |

| | |
|---|---|
| 3 tablespoons khoa (see recipe p. 24) or unsweetened, evaporated milk | |

| | |
|---|---|
| 15 almonds, soaked, peeled and chopped fine | ½ cup raisins |
| 15 pistachio nuts, unsalted or salt washed off | ½ teaspoon vanilla extract |
| | whipped cream (optional garnish) |

1) In a thick-bottomed saucepan, bring the milk to a boil and add the honey, stirring until the honey dissolves. Remove from the heat and set aside.

2) In a large, thick-bottomed frying pan, heat the ghee and fry the cream of wheat, flour and green cardamon seeds until light brown. Add the boiled milk and khoa or evaporated milk, *stirring continuously*, until the mixture is thick. Then mix in the almonds, pistachios and raisins and continue cooking and stirring until the ghee starts to separate out. Then remove from the heat and mix in vanilla extract. Serve hot with a dollop of whipped cream (optional).

Yield: ½-1 cup

# Special Occasion Pudding
## (Raaj Bhog Halwaa)

A sweet, soft cereal dessert — very rich.

| | |
|---|---|
| *⅔ cup honey* | *2 cups water* |

| | |
|---|---|
| *1 cup ghee* | *1 tablespoon pistachio nuts,* |
| *⅔ cup cream of wheat* | *unsalted or salt washed off* |
| *3 black cardamon pods (use* | *1 tablespoon almonds,* |
| *only the seeds)* | *soaked, peeled and* |
| *2 tablespoons garbanzo flour* | *chopped fine* |
| *⅔ cup khoa (see recipe p. 24)* | |
| *or unsweetened,* | |
| *evaporated milk* | |

*2 tablespoons hot ghee*

1) In a thick-bottomed saucepan, bring the honey and water to a boil, cooking until the honey is dissolved.

2) In a thick-bottomed frying pan, heat the ghee and fry the cream of wheat and cardamon seeds. When half fried (slightly brown), stir in the garbanzo flour and continue cooking on a low heat, *stirring continuously*, until golden brown. Then add the honey syrup. Stir well and add the khoa or evaporated milk, pistachios and almonds. Keep cooking and stirring until all the water is absorbed and the ghee starts to separate out. Remove from the heat. Before serving, pour two tablespoons of hot ghee over the pudding. Serve warm!

Yield: 3 cups

# Carrot Pudding
## (Gaajar Kaa Halwaa)

1 cup "half and half" milk

4 medium carrots, washed, peeled and grated

1⅛ cups khoa (see recipe
  p. 24) or unsweetened,
  evaporated milk

2 cups honey
12 raisins
12 almonds, soaked, peeled
  and slivered

12 pistachio nuts, unsalted or
  salt washed off, chopped
1 cup sweet butter

1) In a thick-bottomed saucepan, bring the "half and half" milk to a boil and add the grated carrots. Cook, *stirring continuously*, until the carrots have absorbed all the milk.

2) Add the khoa (or evaporated milk) and continue to cook until most of the moisture evaporates and the mixture has a stiff consistency.

3) Stir in the honey, raisins, almonds, pistachios and sweet butter. Fry until a rich brown in color. Serve hot or cold.

Yield: approximately 3½ cups

# Cream of Wheat Pudding
## (Soojee Kee Kheer)

Nice for breakfast or for dessert.

4 cups milk

| | |
|---|---|
| 2 tablespoons sweet butter | 1 cup cream of wheat |

| | |
|---|---|
| 1/2 teaspoon cardamon powder (optional) | 3/4 cup honey<br>1/2 teaspoon salt |

| | |
|---|---|
| 1 tablespoon pistachios, unsalted or salt washed off, chopped | 1 tablespoon almonds, soaked, peeled and slivered |

1) In a thick-bottomed large saucepan, bring the milk to a boil.

2) In a thick-bottomed frying pan, heat the butter and fry the cream of wheat until slightly brown. Sprinkle cream of wheat and cardamon powder (optional) over the boiling milk and simmer until the mixture becomes very thick and the cream of wheat grains are soft. Stir in the honey and salt.

3) Pour into a tray and decorate with pistachios and almonds.

Yield: 4 cups

# Fragrant Cream of Wheat Pudding
## (Soojee Kaa Halwaa)

A very sweet treat.

| | |
|---|---|
| ¼ cup honey | 1½ cups water |
| ½ cup ghee | ½ cup cream of wheat |
| ¼ cup raisins, rinsed | |

| | |
|---|---|
| ½ teaspoon rose water | 8 pistachio nuts, unsalted or |
| 2 green cardamon pods (use | salt washed off, chopped |
| only the seeds) | a few raisins for garnish |
| 8 almonds, soaked, peeled | |
| and sliced | |

1) In a saucepan, boil the honey and water for 5 minutes.

2) In a large, thick-bottomed frying pan, heat the ghee and, *stirring continuously*, fry the cream of wheat on a low heat until light brown. Then add the honey syrup and the raisins. Continue cooking and stirring until the cream of wheat sweets up, the water is absorbed, and the ghee starts to separate out. Remove from the heat and stir in the rose water. Pour the mixture into a serving dish. Decorate with crushed cardamon seeds, almonds, pistachios and a few more raisins.

Yield: 1-1½ cups

# Royal Toast
## *(Shaahee Tukaree)*

A rich dessert — serve with a light meal, or serve with fruit for breakfast.

| | |
|---|---|
| *8 thick slices of bread* | *2 cups vegetable oil or ghee for deep frying* |

| | |
|---|---|
| *2 cups milk* | *8 green cardamon pods (use* |
| *¾ cup honey* | *only the seeds)* |

| | |
|---|---|
| *⅔ cup khoa (see recipe p. 24) or unsweetened, evaporated milk* | *¼ teaspoon kewra essence* |

| | |
|---|---|
| *1 tablespoon almonds, soaked, peeled and sliced* | *1 teaspoon pistachios, unsalted or salt washed off, chopped* |
| *4 cherries, pitted and chopped* | |
| *6 silver leaves* | |

1) Cut the crusts from the bread and slice diagonally in half. In a thick-bottomed saucepan, heat the oil or ghee for deep frying. Fry the bread slices until golden brown. Remove with a slotted spoon, letting the excess oil drip back into the pan. Drain further on paper towels.

2) In a thick-bottomed saucepan, bring the milk to a boil and turn off the heat. Mix in the honey and green cardamon seeds until the honey dissolves. Soak the deep fried bread in this syrup for 1 minute. Remove from the heat and set aside.

3) In a thick-bottomed saucepan, stir the khoa or evaporated milk into the milk and cook over a low heat, *stirring continuously,* until it thickens a little. Remove from heat and add kewra essence. Soak the bread in this mixture for 2 or 3 minutes, turning each piece over a few times. Remove with a flat spoon or spatula and arrange on a plate.

*For decoration:*
Decorate with sliced almonds, pistachios, cherries and silver leaf. Let cool before serving.

Yield: 16 half-slices

# Nutty Cookies
## (Nan Kataaee)

| | |
|---|---|
| ½ cup honey | 1 teaspoon yogurt |
| ½ cup ghee or melted sweet butter | |

| | |
|---|---|
| 1¾ cups unbleached white flour | ½ teaspoon baking soda |
| | ½ teaspoon baking powder |

| | |
|---|---|
| 2 black cardamon pods (seeds only, crushed) | 40 pistachio nuts, unsalted or salt washed off, chopped |

1) In a bowl, mix together the honey and ghee or melted sweet butter. (This mixture should be cool.) Add the yogurt and stir well.

2) In another bowl, sift together the flour, baking soda and baking powder. Add the dry ingredients to the honey/ghee mixture, stirring to form a thick paste. Form this into small balls, about the size of a walnut. Roll in crushed cardamon and chopped pistachios.

3) Pre-heat the oven to 300 degrees. Place the balls on an oiled cookie sheet and bake until brown. Remove from the oven and cool on a wire rack.

Yield: 2 dozen cookies

# Coconut Pastries
## (Naryaal "Biscuit")

1 tablespoon sweet butter
1 tablespoon ghee

1 tablespoon honey

---

3 teaspoons milk
4 ½ tablespoons unbleached
  white flour, sifted
½ teaspoon baking powder

1 tablespoon coconut powder
¼ cup flour for dusting pastry
  board

1) In a bowl, beat together the butter, ghee and honey. Then stir in the milk, sifted flour, baking powder and coconut powder. Mix thoroughly to form a dough.

2) On a lightly floured pastry board or flat surface, roll the dough out to ½ inch thickness. Cut with a cookie cutter. Pre-heat the oven to 350 degrees. Place the cookies on the cookie sheet and bake for 10 minutes, until golden brown. Cool on a wire rack.

Yield: 12 one-inch square cookies

# Fruit Cake

1½ cups khoa (see recipe
  p. 24) or unsweetened,
  evaporated milk
1 cup water
3 tablespoons melted sweet
  butter or ghee

½ teaspoon vanilla extract
½ teaspoon lemon extract

---

2 cups unbleached white flour
¾ cup fructose or raw sugar
3 teaspoons baking powder
¾ teaspoon baking soda
¼ teaspoon powdered
  cinnamon

¼ teaspoon powdered ginger
pinch of salt
¾ cup assorted dried fruit,
  chopped

1) In a bowl, mix together the khoa or evaporated milk, water, melted butter or ghee, vanilla and lemon extract. In another bowl, sift together the flour, fructose or raw sugar, baking powder, baking

soda, powdered cinnamon, powdered ginger, and salt. Add the dry ingredients to the liquid, mixing thoroughly. Then add the dried fruits and mix again.

2) Pre-heat the oven to 350 degrees. Oil a bread pan and pour in the batter. Bake for 30-40 minutes.

Yield: 1 loaf

# Pineapple Cake

For the cake:

| | |
|---|---|
| 2 tablespoons butter at room temperature | 1/4 teaspoon pineapple extract |
| | 1/4 cup milk |
| 3 tablespoons condensed milk (presweetened) | 1/2 cup honey |

| | |
|---|---|
| 1 1/4 cups white unbleached flour | 1 teaspoon baking powder |
| | 1/4 teaspoon baking soda |

| | |
|---|---|
| 1 teaspoon vegetable oil or ghee to oil pan | 1 tablespoon flour to dust pan |

For the decoration:

| | |
|---|---|
| 1/2 cup honey | 1/4 teaspoon pineapple extract |
| 1/4 cup non-instant powdered milk | 1/4 cup canned pineapple juice |

| | |
|---|---|
| 3 slices canned pineapple, chopped | 1/2 cup walnuts, chopped |
| a few cherries, pitted and chopped | |

To make the cake:

1) Set out butter at room temperature for 1 hour (until soft).

2) In a bowl, beat together the butter, condensed milk, pineapple extract, milk and honey. In another bowl, sift together the flour, baking powder and baking soda. Add the dry ingredients to the liquid, stirring thoroughly.

191

3) Pre-heat the oven to 300 degrees. Oil a 9 by 12 inch pan with melted ghee or vegetable oil and dust lightly with flour. Pour the cake batter into the tray and bake until a toothpick inserted into the cake comes out clean. Remove from the oven and cool on a wire rack. Take the cake out of the tray, wrap in a cloth, and store in an airtight container for at least 4 hours.

*To decorate:*
1) Beat together honey and powdered milk, and then add pineapple extract and pineapple juice until slightly thick. (This icing soaks through the cake, giving it a moist, sweet taste. For a drier cake, heat the icing till it thickens.)

2) Cut the cake in half. Spread each layer with the pineapple icing and sprinkle with chopped pineapple bits. Place one layer on top of the other. Garnish the top with cherries and walnuts.

Yield: One 9 x 6 x 2 inch cake

## Candy:

# Coconut Fudge
## (Naryaal Barfee)

2¼ cups khoa (see recipe p. 24) or unsweetened, evaporated milk

2 tablespoons water

---

1½ cups fructose or 1½ cups honey and a scant pinch of baking soda

½ cup coconut, shredded

2 teaspoons water (optional)
a little beet juice for coloring
3 silver leaves for decoration

1) In a thick-bottomed frying pan, cook the khoa or evaporated milk and water on a low heat, *stirring continuously*. Add the sweetener and continue cooking and stirring until the mixture will not stick to your fingertip. Remove from the heat and let it cool. Then stir in the coconut. If the mixture is too thick, stir in 2 teaspoons of water.

2) Separate the mixture into two parts. In one part, mix in enough beet juice to turn it pink. Sprinkle some water on a platter and spread the white portion out on it evenly. Then spread the pink portion evenly over that. Decorate with silver leaf. Cool in the refrigerator until set. Cut into small pieces before serving.

Note: If honey is substituted for solid sweetener in this recipe, the consistency will be that of soft, somewhat sticky fudge. Beat persistently during cooking to minimize this effect.

Yield: 8 by 10 inch sheet of fudge

# Quick Pistachio-Almond Fudge
## (Pistaa-Badaam Barfee)

Quick and very rich.

4½ cups (2 pounds)
  condensed milk (presweet-
  ened)

| 1 tablespoon sweet butter | 20 pistachios, unsalted or salt |
| 10 almonds, soaked, peeled | washed off |
| and slivered | 2 silver leaves |

1) In a thick-bottomed frying pan, cook the condensed milk on a low heat, *stirring continuously* with a wire whisk and scraping the bottom frequently to prevent burning, until light brown in color and very thick.

2) Butter a cookie sheet with the sweet butter and pour in the condensed milk. Decorate the top with almonds and pistachios. Let cool and set (you may wish to refrigerate for extra firmness), then decorate with silver leaf. Cut this very sweet confection into very small pieces before serving.

Yield: 11 by 15 inch sheet of (thin) fudge

# Almond Fudge
## (Badaam Barfee)

3 tablespoons almonds,
  soaked and peeled, or
  almond powder
3 tablespoons fructose or 3
  tablespoons honey and a
  scant pinch of baking soda

3 tablespoons water
1 tablespoon vegetable oil or
  ghee for frying
2½ tablespoons khoa (see
  recipe p. 24) or unsweetened, evaporated milk

---

1-2 drops kewra essence

1 teaspoon vegetable oil to oil
  plate

---

silver leaf for decoration

1) Grind the almonds to the consistency of meal, either in an electric blender or coffee mill *or* use almond powder.

2) Dissolve the sweetener in the water and cook it on a low heat, being careful not to scorch, until a sticky syrup is formed.

3) In a thick-bottomed frying pan, heat the oil or ghee and fry the khoa or evaporated milk on a low heat, *stirring continuously*, until light brown (approximately 4 minutes) and oil or ghee is just starting to separate out. Then remove from heat, add almonds, syrup and kewra essence and mix well.

4) Spread this mixture out on an oiled plate and *let set for 3 or 4 hours* in refrigerator. Before serving, decorate with silver leaf and cut into small pieces.

Yield: 9 small pieces

# Creamy Mixed Fruit Bark
## (Pistaa Barfee)

A chewy, nutty confection. The cardamon adds a touch of the exotic.

| | |
|---|---|
| 3 cups khoa (see recipe p. 24) or unsweetened, evaporated milk | 1/2 cup fructose or 1/2 cup honey and a pinch of baking soda |

| | |
|---|---|
| 2 tablespoons almonds, soaked, peeled and chopped | 6 green cardamon pods (use only the seeds) |
| 2 tablespoons pistachios, unsalted or salt washed off, chopped | 1 teaspoon vegetable oil to oil cookie sheet |
| | 3 silver leaves |

1) In a thick-bottomed saucepan, mix together the khoa or evaporated milk and sweetener and cook over a low heat until the sweetener is dissolved. Then remove from the heat and *beat well* with a spoon. Return to the heat and continue to cook, *stirring continuously*. When the mixture no longer feels sticky to your fingertip, add the almonds, pistachios and cardamon seeds and stir.

2) Spread the mixture out evenly on an oiled cookie sheet. Let sit 3 or 4 hours to set. Decorate with silver leaf and cut into small pieces before serving.

Yield: 4 by 8 inch sheet of (thin) candy

# Creamy Orange Candy
## *(Kalaa Kand)*

*¹⁄₃ cup lemon peels*

---

*2 tablespoons melted ghee*
*3¹⁄₂ cups (1¹⁄₂ pounds) khoa
(see recipe p. 24) or
unsweetened, evaporated
milk*

*¹⁄₂ cup fructose or ¹⁄₃ cup
honey and a scant pinch of
baking soda*
*¹⁄₂ cup milk*

---

*¹⁄₂ teaspoon orange extract*

1) Wash and peel the lemons. Chop the peels into small pieces.

2) In a thick-bottomed frying pan, mix together the ghee, khoa or evaporated milk, sweetener, lemon peel and milk and cook on a low heat, *stirring continuously*, until dry and sticky. Stir in the orange extract. Remove from the heat and spread the mixture out on a platter or cookie sheet. Let it cool until set. Cut into small pieces before serving.

Yield: 4 by 8 inch sheet of (thin) candy

# Coconut Squares
## *(Naryaal Tikkee)*

A fast simple treat.

*3 slices whole wheat bread*
*½ cup unsweetened, evapor-*
*ated milk*

*2 tablespoons honey*
*¼ teaspoon salt*
*¼ cup dry, grated coconut*

1) Cut the crusts from the bread. Cut each slice of bread into quarters.

2) Mix together the evaporated milk, honey and salt. Dip each piece of bread into this mixture. Then sprinkle the top with grated coconut.

3) Pre-heat the oven to 350 degrees. Place the bread on a wire rack, coconut side up, and bake until golden brown. Serve hot.

Yield: 12 squares

*Story:*

# The Guru's Lesson

Guru Gobind Singh taught that each person should think of his own home as a free kitchen. Whatever food was in his cupboard did not truly "belong" to him; it was merely in his custody to be used to feed whoever might be in need.

The Guru decided to test his disciples to see how well they were practicing hospitality as he taught it. Disguised as a lowly beggar, he went to their homes late in the evenings and humbly requested some food. When his survey was complete, he gathered his congregation together and made his report:

"I'm glad to say that in none of the homes I visited was the 'lowly beggar' turned away empty handed. Even the least gracious among you asked him to wait at the door while you fetched some leftover breads or sweets for him to take on his way.

"Those who were more generous invited the man to come in. They explained that they had no food ready, but bade him wait while they fixed something.

"But the true spirit of the free kitchen was only practiced by one man, my disciple Nand Lal. When the beggar arrived at his door, he welcomed him in the name of God and asked him to come in. Then he quickly went to the kitchen and returned carrying a sack of wheat, a sack of beans and a container of yogurt. 'Kind sir,' he said, 'all of this food is yours for God has provided it. Now please be kind enough to let me prepare it for you.' "

# Special Ingredients
# and Where To Find Them

Indian cooking is most enjoyable when your kitchen is well stocked with the spices and ingredients that give Indian cuisine its distinctive flavors. Here is a list of items that you are not likely to find in your local supermarket, what they are, their Indian names, and mail order sources, if known.

Following the list of ingredients is a partial listing of specialty food stores throughout North America that stock a variety of Indian ingredients.

ASAFOETIDA, *hing.* Old herbal texts call it "Devil's dung;" it does have a fairly "fetid" (rotten) smell, hence its name. Upon frying, in oil, it undergoes a magical transformation and takes on an onion-like flavor. Made from the juices of plants of the fennel family, it is used medicinally as an anti-spasmodic.

BASMATI *(basmaatee)* RICE, a special long-grained, aromatic white unpolished rice imported from India. "Texmati," a North American rice, is a good substitute.

BITTER MELON, karelaa, a small, green, bumpy-skinned, cucumber-shaped melon.

CARDAMON, *ilaaechee.* A highly aromatic spice, it comes in pods, seeds or ground. The pods come in two colors, *green* and *black* or dark brown. (The white pods are just green pods that have been bleached). The little black seeds are used, the pods discarded. *Where recipes require black cardamon, green can be substituted.*

CHAPATI FLOUR, *aattaa;* a finely ground whole wheat flour similar to whole wheat pastry flour. "Golden Temple Chapati Flour" can be ordered by phone or mail from Spice and Sweet Mahal Store, 135 Lexington Ave., New York, NY 10016, 212-683-0900.

CHICKPEA FLOUR, *besan;* also known as gram flour or garbanzo flour.

CINNAMON, *daalcheenee;* literally means "sweet wood;" the dried, inner bark of an evergreen tree of the laurel family; it comes rolled in short sticks (quills), bark chips, or ground. Stick cinnamon is available in some supermarkets.

CITRIC ACID, *nimboo kaa sar;* used to split milk into curds and whey in the making of panir; *tartaric acid or lemon juice may be substituted;* also available in powdered form.

CORIANDER, *dhaneeaa,* (cilantro, Chinese parsley); very distinctive, pleasant, slightly pungent taste; used as fresh leaves, seeds and ground. Available in many supermarkets.

CUMIN, *jeeraa.* A strongly aromatic and slightly nutty spice, it comes in three types — *white, black* or *brown* — and is used either whole or ground. *White cumin is the most commonly used and may be substituted for the less common varieties.*

DAHL, *daal,* describes all varieties of beans. Specialty shops may stock a dozen or more varieties in bulk. Be sure to clean and rinse thoroughly before using.

FENUGREEK, *methee;* small, triangle shaped seeds with a licorice-like flavor; used whole or ground. Available in many supermarkets.

GINGER, *adrak.* Often referred to as a root, ginger is actually a "rhizome." Use whole, dried or ground. Available in many supermarkets.

KEWRA ESSENCE, *rooh kewra;* a highly fragrant essence of the screw pine; used for desserts; available in bottles from specialty stores as "kewra water."

LOTUS ROOT, *kanwal kakree;* the root of the lotus flower; available peeled and canned from specialty stores; may be ordered by phone or mail from India Spice and Gift Bazaar, 3060 Clairemont Drive, San Diego, CA 92117, 619-276-7226. A 14-ounce can is roughly equivalent to 4 six-inch-long roots.

MANGO POWDER, *ambchoor;* used as a souring agent, like lemon juice; made from unripe mangoes, peeled, dried and powdered.

MUSTARD OIL, a hot, aromatic oil, used for pickles.

NUTMEG, *jaiphal;* can be obtained whole from specialty stores. Grind with mortar and pestle, electric grinder or food processor.

POMEGRANATE POWDER, *anaardaanaa*; the dried, powdered seeds of the pomegranate, also known as the Chinese apple; used as a sweet and sour agent.

RICE POWDER, used as a thickener. *Substitute corn starch or whole wheat pastry flour.*

SAFFRON, *kesar;* a yellow aromatic spice made from the stigmas of crocus flowers; also, the world's most expensive spice!

SANDALWOOD ESSENCE, an aromatic essence of the sandalwood tree, available in bottles.

SILVER LEAF, *vark;* a decorative foil which contains pure silver. It is edible and is believed to have medicinal properties.

TAMARIND, *imlee;* the sweet and sour fruit of a tropical tree. It comes in a paste with the seeds still in it, or in a seedless concentrate; used as a sweet-sour agent.

TARTARIC ACID, *imlee kaa sat;* a souring agent, used for splitting milk in curds and whey when making panir; citric acid or lemon juice can be substituted.

WHITE PEPPER. If unavailable, substitute the more common black variety.

WHITE POPPY SEEDS, *khaskhas.* Raw, they are odorless, tasteless and off-white; ground, they smell much like roasted sesame oil; used as a thickening agent.

The following stores stock many of the items listed above. Most of them will be happy to accept your orders by phone or mail. If you're unfamiliar with Indian ingredients, you might request that the items you order be carefully labeled *in English.* Stores are listed alphabetically by state, city and store name.

**ALABAMA**
Golden Temple Emporium
1901 11th Ave. So.
Birmingham, AL 35205

**ARIZONA**
Golden Temple Health Center
109 E. Southern
Tempe, AZ 85283

**CALIFORNIA**
Bazaar of India
1810 University Ave.
Berkeley, CA 94703

Bombay Bazaar
1034 University Ave.
Berkeley, CA 94701

Villa's Market
1912 Arrow Highway
LaVerne, CA 91750

Berjian Grocery
4725 Santa Monica Blvd.
Los Angeles, CA 90029

Golden Temple Foods
1639 So. La Cienega
Los Angeles, CA 90048

India Bazaar
11415 W. Washington Blvd.
Los Angeles, CA 90066

India Food Mill
650 E. San Bruno Ave.
San Bruno, CA 94066
(415)583-6559

India Spice and Gift Bazaar
3060 Clairemont Drive
San Diego, CA 92117

Haig's Delicacies
642 Clement St.
San Francisco, CA 94118

India Gifts and Foods
643 Post St.
San Francisco, CA 94109

Bharat Bazaar
3680 El Camino Real
Santa Clara, CA 95051

## ILLINOIS
India Groceries
5022 No. Sheridan Rd.
Chicago, IL 60640

## LOUISIANA
Central Grocery
923 Decatur St.
New Orleans, LA 70116

## MASSACHUSETTS
Cambridge Coffee, Tea and
Spices
1765 Massachusetts Ave.
Cambridge, MA 02138

## MARYLAND
The Golden Temple Center
2322 N. Charles
Baltimore, MD 21218

Indian Sub-Continental Store
908 Philadelphia Ave.
Silver Springs, MD 20910

## MISSOURI
Indian Food Center
15-43 McCausland Ave.
St. Louis, MO 63117

## NEW YORK
Annapurna
127 E. 28th St.
New York, NY 10016

Foods of India
Sinha Trading Co., Inc.
120 Lexington Ave.
New York, NY 10016
(212)683-4419

Little India Store
128 E. 28th St.
New York, NY 10016

Pete's Spice and Everything Nice
174 First Ave.
New York, NY 10009

Spice and Sweet Mahal Store
135 Lexington Ave.
New York, NY 10016

## NEVADA
Golden Temple Foods
902 So. Virginia
Reno, NV 89502
702-786-4110

## OKLAHOMA
Antone's
2606 Sheridan
Tulsa, OK 74129

Golden Temple Natural Foods
2504 N. Military
Oklahoma City, OK 73106

## OREGON
Porter's Foods Unlimited
125 W. 11th Ave.
Eugene, OR 97401

## PENNSYLVANIA

Avatar's Golden Nectar
321 Bridge St.
New Cumberland, PA 17070

Indian Super Bazaar
4101 Walnut St.
Philadelphia, PA 19104

## TEXAS

Antone's Import Company
4234 Harry Hines Blvd.
Dallas, TX 75219

Mahalaxmi Mills
5721 Savoy Ln.
Houston, TX 77036
(713)782-9911

## VERMONT

Origanum
247 Main St.
Burlington, VT 05401

## WASHINGTON

House of Rice
4122 University Way N.E.
Seattle, WA 98105

## ONTARIO, CANADA

Top Banana Ltd.
1526 Merivale Rd.
Ottawa, ONT
Canada

Golden Temple Products
468 Bloor Street West
Toronto, ONT M5S 1X8
Canada

Indo-Canada
624 Bloor St., West
Toronto, ONT
Canada

Indo-Canada
1453 Gerrard East
Toronto, ONT
Canada

Punjab Grocers
2077 Davenport Rd.
Toronto, ONT
Canada

Sharma Grocery Store
2800 Bundas St., West
Toronto, ONT
Canada

# Index

# About the Author

Bibiji Inderjit Kaur was born in 1935 in India (now West Pakistan). As the daughter of a devoted Sikh family, she grew up steeped in the Sikh traditions of community and service. She studied at Punjab University and later completed her M.A. at the University of New Mexico in Albuquerque and will soon complete her Ph.D. at the University of Humanistic Studies in San Diego, California, in marriage and family counseling.

When she was eighteen years old, she married the world renowned yogi and religious leader Siri Singh Sahib Bhai Sahib Dr. Harbhajan Singh Khalsa Yogiji, affectionately known to the world as Yogi Bhajan. They have raised two beautiful sons and one daughter who enthusiastically attest to her remarkable homemaking skills. She has amazed their many friends with her capacity to create gourmet delights for hundreds of guests. She has served the poor and heads of states alike with grace, dignity and a pleasant, charming personality that make her a truly exceptional hostess.

In addition to teaching the art of Indian cooking, Bibiji, as she is called, is active as a psychological and family counselor. She holds the esteemed position of chief minister for religious affairs of the Sikh Dharma in the West. She has been the recipient of many awards for her outstanding community service, including proclamations from Governor Bruce King of New Mexico and Congressman Bill Richardson of Washington, D.C.

Bibiji has taught cooking classes all over the country, including appearances on local television stations. Her several occupations keep her traveling here and abroad as teacher, counselor and goodwill ambassador. Her greatest joy, however, remains the time she can spend cooking and sharing with her husband, children and grandchildren.

# Other Books of Interest

## The Golden Temple Vegetarian Cookbook
By Yogi Bhajan. Gourmet vegetarian recipes from the world-famous chain of Golden Temple restaurants. Soups, salads, beverages, breads, entrees and wonderful desserts. 224 pp. $8.50.

## Conscious Cookery
By Siri Ved Kaur Khalsa. No vegetarian cook should be without this book. An essential collection of gourmet recipes just waiting to come to life in your kitchen. Also includes traditional healing recipes from India. 98pp. $6.95.

## Foods for Health & Healing: Remedies & Recipes
Based on the teachings of Yogi Bhajan. A new way to health and happiness based on ancient ayurvedic and yogic medicine. Yogi Bhajan shows how food is our best medicine. *Foods For Health & Healing* presents the basics of good nutrition and good eating habits as well as common and uncommon remedies, diets, fasts and over 50 unique healing recipes. 144pp. illus. $6.95.

## The New Consciousness Sourcebook
Features information and addresses of thousands of new age centers, schools and businesses. Health, meditation, therapy, bodywork, movement, occult, nutrition and more . . . . Articles and illustrations. The *Whole Life Times* says, "*The New Consciousness Sourcebook*, is the reference book by which all related networking publications must be measured." 256pp. illus. $8.95.

## The Teachings of Yogi Bhajan
By Yogi Bhajan. The affirmations, wit and wisdom of Yogi Bhajan, Ph.D., provide a practical demonstration of the power of the spoken word. His words on Love, Happiness, God, Mind and Relationships cut through negative mind states and help to restore a positive mental attitude. Yogi Bhajan, Master of Kundalini Yoga and founder of the science of humanology, has helped hundreds of thousands of individuals to learn meditation and thus experience the fullness of life. 193pp. $8.95.

## Yoga for the 80's.
Kundalini Yoga as taught by Yogi Bhajan. Here's the latest collection of joyful, dynamic exercises, drawn from ancient tradition to meet the challenges of life in the 80's. Increase your stamina and creativity. Learn the art of calmness in a crisis. Build strength to persevere in spite of all obstacles. Stay vigorously young! Clearly illustrated in a cheerful workbook format. 36pp. illus. $6.95.

TO ORDER: Send check or money order in U.S. dollars to *K.R.I. Publications, PO Box 1550, Pomona, CA 91769.* Include $1.50 for the first book and $.50 for each additional book to cover shipping and handling. California residents add 6½ percent sales tax.